Radical

Rapport

GOD REALLY DOES SPEAK TO US

BY: B.J. PERES

Romeo,
Thank you for all the great
teaching. Loved your
class. In Him,
B.J.
Phil 1:3

I DEDICATE THIS BOOK TO:

MY MENTOR, SYLVIA LAFOND, WHO IS ALWAYS THERE FOR ME. I AM ASTOUNDED BY THE AMAZING SPIRITUAL GIFTS WITH WHICH SHE HAS BEEN BESTOWED. WHETHER I AM HURTING, NEED PRAYER, AM TROUBLED AND IN NEED OF AN EXPLANATION FOR SOMETHING, CONFUSED AND IN NEED OF GOD'S MIND ON SOMETHING, OR JUST IN NEED OF A FRIEND WHO IS A COMBINATION OF A SPIRITUAL MOTHER, SISTER, TEACHER, CONFIDANT AND ALL THE ABOVE, SHE IS ALWAYS THERE FOR ME. I RESPECT HER HONESTY AND TRUST HER WISDOM AND KNOWLEDGE AS NOTHING LESS THAN THAT OF THE LORD'S. SHE IS A FAITHFUL SUPPORTER. SHE HAS BEEN HAND-PICKED BY GOD TO HELP ME THROUGH LIFE'S JOURNEY ENABLING ME TO EXPERIENCE PEACE, REST AND HAPPINESS;

MY GIRLFRIENDS: JOAN GRAY, CHRISTINE FARLING, ELAINE COY AND ANDREA GILPATRICK WHO HAVE ENRICHED MY LIFE WITH THEIR LOVE AND FELLOWSHIP...

JOAN HAS BEEN MY FAITHFUL FRIEND SINCE OUR SONS WERE LITTLE AND IN CUB SCOUTS. WE WORKED AT A HEALTH CLUB TOGETHER AND WENT TO CHURCH TOGETHER. SHE HELPED ME TO RE-LOCATE WHEN I MOVED TO MARYLAND, AND WAS EVEN INSTRUMENTAL IN SHIPPING PACKAGES TO MY NEW ADDRESS. SHE DROVE ME TO CANADA A FEW TIMES WHEN I WENT ON ADVENTURES. SHE WAS THE ONLY ONE WHO WROTE TO ME WHEN I WAS OVERSEAS. I STAYED AT HER HOME FOR WEEKS ON END EACH TIME I RETURNED FROM THE MISSION FIELD. WE HAVE GONE OUT FOR LUNCH AND DINNER NUMEROUS TIMES OVER THE YEARS ENJOYING MANY HOURS OF SWEET FELLOWSHIP. SHE IS ALWAYS BRINGING ME STUFF--ORANGES FROM FLORIDA, PIZZA STUFFERS, HEALTHY SNACKS AND YOU NAME IT. SHE IS A TRUE CONFIDANT. I CANNOT IMAGINE MY LIFE WITHOUT HER...

MY FRIENDSHIP WITH CHRISITNE IS VERY DEEP. WE ONLY HAD THE PLEASURE OF LIVING NEAR ONE ANOTHER AND GOING TO THE SAME CHURCH FOR A FEW YEARS; NEVERTHELESS, WE HAVE REMAINED DEAR FRIENDS THROUGH LETTERS, CARDS, THE INTERNET AND IRREGULAR VISITS WHEN SHE VISITS NEW ENGLAND. NO MATTER HOW MANY OR HOW FEW WORDS ARE COMMUNICATED BETWEEN US, THEY GO TO THE DEPTHS OF OUR SOUL. SHE CONTINUALLY EDIFIES AND ENCOURAGES ME. I KNOW WHAT DAVID FELT FOR JONATHAN BECAUSE OF MY FRIENDSHIP WITH CHRISTINE...

ELAINE AND I SHARE THE SAME ITALIAN HERITAGE WHICH PROVIDES THE OPPORTUNITY TO STEP OUT OF MY AMERICAN CULTURE TO REVISIT THE WAYS OF MY ETHNICITY VIA EXPRESSIONS--VOCAL AND BODY--AND TO ALIGN WITH ONE ANOTHER'S THINKING. BEING FROM THE SAME BACKGROUND, WE TOTALLY 'GET' EACH OTHER. HER LOVE FOR GOD PERMEATES MY HOUSE WHEN SHE IS HERE. SHE ALWAYS CRIES WHEN I SING. SHE IS A GIFT...

ANDREA IS MORE LIKE FAMILY THAN A FRIEND. WE GO BACK TO THE EARLY 70'S. I WAS BY HER SIDE WHEN SHE WENT THROUGH A LIVING NIGHTMARE. I WATCHED HER FIGHT GIANTS AND COME OUT VICTORIOUS. I WAS HER MATRON OF HONOR WHEN THINGS LOOKED UP FOR HER AND SHE RE-MARRIED. SHE HAS INSPIRED ME MANY TIMES OVER. I'VE WATCHED GOD TRANSFORM HER JUST AS SHE HAS WATCHED HIM TRANSFORM ME. SHE IS A ROCK. HER LOVE FOR ME GIVES ME STRENGTH.

INTRODUCTION

To say that the work I have been put on earth to accomplish is anything less than an opus would be to sabotage God's calling on my life. I use the word 'accomplish' not as in working or exercising any physical energy of my own, but as in being available to God to manifest Himself through me. Like Mr. Holland's (opus) my life's circumstances led me in a different direction than I would have pursued on my own; still, God has been the ultimate Planner in the production of my life's story--all acts and scenes. My life's ambition has always been to write a story of my life; the book has not been encapsulated in any of God's plans for me (at least not yet). His plan for me has been to be available to Him to minister God's love and grace to people, and to be used by Him to bring about inner healing in men and women.

His plan for me also includes writing testimonies about what He has done in my life which ultimately is far greater than anything that I or anyone else could write. Part of that plan includes bringing my testimonies home to my readers incorporating each person into my life and more importantly into His life. It is they who have impressed upon me that they have been able to put themselves into every situation I describe because I am describing their lives as well. Thank you, readers. Ultimately, His plan for me is to walk with Him, to be pleasing to Him and to fellowship with Him all my days.

For the Lord to have invested in me, an introverted, tiny person with an inferiority complex who was forced to get married at the age of 16 followed by a course of hopelessness for years on end, and to have faithfully granted me patience, tolerance, help, encouragement and hope as fragile, immature and clueless as I was is beyond my human comprehension. I don't need to comprehend it though, I just need to receive this life, to walk in it, to abide in His Son. Slowly, but surely, I came to know Him. To know Him is to love Him, and I do love Him. Once we truly come to know God we will desire to emulate Him; this is my desire. At long last I think I have come to know Him in the way He desires to be known, and I believe that at the present point in my life I have experienced the ultimate abandonment from the world for the cause of His Son renouncing all for His kingdom. If this is not the case, I pray that I will not be lax in achieving the ultimate abandonment before He calls me home.

Writing is a calling. It not only requires time, money, energy, steadfastness and perseverance, it requires a person's whole being. Someone once wrote that an author never has a vacation. He is a walking sponge, sopping up impressions till he is saturated, then going to his desk and squeezing them out on paper. I, personally, can't even sit back to enjoy an uninterrupted movie, the reason being that every few minutes during the show I have to pull myself away from the theater screen, T.V. screen or computer monitor to write down impressionable facts, words, trivia and thoughts that I may be able to incorporate into my work in the future-- not performing that function would make me crazy--as if the impressions would be floating into the atmosphere lost forever.

It has also been said that writing is like a nursery to a botanist. To me it is like breathing or walking. God compels me to write. He gives me the thoughts, I write them down, and then He replenishes me with new thoughts.

My former publications contain over 1,000 personal Christian testimonies, stories, thoughts and records of my dialogue with God. I have never made a profit from any of my books or booklets.

Complete surrender is a monumentally difficult path. Giving up our will for His will is not even possible lest He accomplish it through us. I try to forget the pain involved in surrendering to God's perfect will, especially when its ugly head surfaces from time to time, yet remaining ever cognizant that the results of such a painstaking journey have produced the utmost satisfaction imaginable, causing me to soar in the abundant life that God created for me. God has done it for many others and He has done it for me; I am eternally grateful. The more He increases, the more I decrease. I can say unashamedly, unabashedly and irrevocably that my Beloved is mine and I am His.

Regarding the time spent studying, writing, sharing Christ with others and counseling, it has been said that when we are around Jesus Christ all the time, we reflect His glory all the time. That sounds good to me. People do not come into the world merely to live, for that is no better than being an animal. We have a spirit, soul and body. To fail to accomplish the purpose for which God destined us is to miss the real joy of life.

God's voice is a most amazing gift to His children. Possessing a super sensitivity to His voice is my greatest treasure on earth. It is and always will be inconceivable to me that He would participate in my, at times, seemingly dull existence making known to me His caring and yearning for my friendship, and making known to me that He sees deep into my soul. He communicates with me 'RADICALLY' pertaining to a sphere of subjects simply because I am His friend. How often? The answer is: As often as I choose for Him to communicate with me, and as often as He chooses to communicate with me. It is continuous; He never tires of it. The continuity of His messages never ceases to leave me baffled as to 'why' and 'why me' until He reminds me that He chooses the uncommon to confound the enemy, and He chooses those who are productive and not lazy, who, no matter how much they have on their plate, will propagate His Word. He also reminds me of the increased glory He receives through the lives of those that the world would least expect to be used of Him.

I cherish His voice. I welcome every word and every syllable that He communicates. His voice is like sweetness personified. Do you hear His voice? Do you perceive that His still, small voice is infiltrating your human spirit? Do you hear the clarity of His voice, or do you brush it off as if thoughts are coming from your inner person? Do you give credence to the Holy Spirit Who lives in God's children? Do you hear what I hear?

God's love is radical; God's forgiveness is radical; all of God's characteristics are radical. Why shouldn't His rapport with us be radical as well?

My prayer is that my readers find this book as good company--full of Godly spirituality, practicality, insights, hope, understanding and comradeship, graced with pleasant conversation without loquacity.

May God bless you all…

TABLE OF CONTENTS

TITLE

CHAPTER 1

BLESSINGS

A GOOD REPORT

I am going to embark on this book of testimonies with a story involving a recipient of my last book, "The First Strawberry is Ripe". The title of the book evolved when Barbara, a woman from Germany who was in my Bible study group, shared a story about when she was a little girl. She had two older brothers, and because she was the only girl in the family, she was deemed her daddy's little princess. One morning when she was still asleep her father tip-toed into her room and shook her ever so gently whispering these words, "the first strawberry is ripe," referring to the first strawberry in the strawberry patch that year. I could scarcely fathom that kind of closeness between a father and a daughter. My emotions reeled as I tried to visualize the tender scene.

God had visited me upon awakening that morning, and His presence was still with me at the ladies' gathering. His lengthy visitation was exceptionally rare causing me to want to cling tightly to the sensation that enveloped me. At the ladies gathering Barbara's words about her dad wanting to take her to the strawberry patch to behold the first strawberry of the season caused my magnetism to God's Spirit to escalate making me reflect on all the unparalleled ways that God whispers His words of love to us. My physical body was at my mentor's house on a beautiful lake in Maine, but my spirit was afar off. I was basking in the Lord. His utterances penetrated all the way to my soul encompassing my entire being.

I knew instantaneously that Barbara's words about the strawberry would be written across the cover of the book I had been writing. I was not forthright with her with the decisive conclusion I had come to regarding the title. I was going to wait and surprise her when the book was published. As fate would have it, I never had that chance; she passed away unexpectedly. She was not sick, nor did she have any threatening medical conditions; God just called her home. Within the next couple of days three of her friends from her church had dreams of Barbara eating strawberries (unbeknownst to them that she loved strawberries). Having heard about a testimony I had written about Barbara, one of the women called me and asked if I would read my strawberry testimony along with reading their stories about her at her memorial service. Although I was scheduled to be on T.V. that same morning and could not attend, and someone else was asked to read for me, it was, nevertheless, an honor to have been asked.

"The First Strawberry is Ripe" was published in November of 2011. Two weeks before Christmas my mentor, Sylvia, entreated me to autograph a copy of my book which she gift wrapped and delivered to Barbara's husband Neil's house one day. He was not there so she left it where it would be in plain sight when he arrived home. The following day Sylvia called to tell me that Neil called her and was in tears as he told her that he had never received anything so meaningful and beautiful. He wanted to thank her, and he wanted her to extend his thankfulness to me for him. The more emotional he became the more he cried so he had to end the conversation. He communicated to her that he would write her a letter to finish telling her what was on his heart.

This occurrence demonstrates the broad meaning of what being an instrument of God entails on this earth. The written word was used as an anesthetic to soothe a distraught husband who was grieving. Sylvia and I had the sacred privilege of ministering Christ to Neil. Ultimately, we could never have done what the Holy Spirit did for him. God was in charge of that.

THE CLUBHOUSE

My church Body and I prayed for 10 months before I moved to Brunswick that God would open the door for a Bible study when I arrived there. Everything went according to our plan in rapid succession after I arrived at my new apartment, plus God went above and beyond what we could ever expect or think. My pastor and his wife made their first one and a half hour trip to my house bringing in their van five church members to my apartment. That was a nice shot in the arm for my homesickness. I kindled excitement for the chance to invite some old friends and some new neighbors to our first Bible study which turned out to exceed our highest expectations. It was a blessed time, indeed. The only problem was that my small living room was not big enough to accommodate comfortably everyone in attendance. With two sofas, a rocker and a living room chair, my dinette chairs and a hassock there was a place for everyone to sit; yet, we were packed in like little fishies in a can. I certainly would not be able to invite anybody else which would have prohibited the growth of our study.

A huge community room/clubhouse was situated diagonally across from my apartment. It was beautifully designed with a cathedral ceiling and wooden beams positioned diagonally throughout. A lovely variety of bright plants graced the front of the building in front of the extended span of windows. A dozen of round tables, each decorated with a handmade decoration relating to the season of year, occupied the large space. In my way of thinking it would have been a shame if the spacious room was left unoccupied the nights that we were to get together for our Bible studies and fellowship. I suggested to those in attendance that we all spend the next couple of weeks praying for God to open a door for us to be able to use the beautiful facility for our gatherings. My friend, Denise, who had sung professionally in a group with her uncles and cousin in previous years, spoke up and said that she could possibly get her family to agree to start singing again, thereby giving free concerts at the clubhouse simultaneously with our fellowship and devotionals. God was surely full of surprises that night.

Two days later I happened to be across the street at the office when I met my new friend, Tom, who happened to be the president of the board at the complex. I told him what I had in mind regarding the use of the clubhouse, and that I wanted to approach the director about it. "How do you think I will make out if I go into his office and talk to him about it?" I asked him. With a hand signal he beckoned me to leave it all up to him. I sat on a comfortable chair in the complex lobby as Tom sauntered into the director's office. Some unusual antiques displayed on a nearby table held my attention momentarily, yet I could not get my focus off a possible let down.

I was not resting in faith rest as I should have been, but was on pins and needles as Tom approached the head honcho on my behalf. I was inundated with thoughts of how utterly perfect it would be to congregate there and to open our concerts to the public. Ten minutes later Tom exited the office giving me a thumbs up. "It's all set. The only stipulation is that you have to agree to open the event to everyone who lives here." Praise God! Aroused with glorious excitement I jumped out of the chair high-fiving Tom and thanking him. It turned out that we would not be charged rent; the management would advertise the events to be held on the last Saturday night of every month in the monthly bulletins which they would pass out to all the residents of the complex. And, if that wasn't enough, Rosie, one of the women who reside in the building, would make and serve coffee to all concert go-ers...all for free. As per usual, God went above and beyond that for which we had prayed.

The concerts have been going on without a hitch for going on two years at this writing. The months that my pastor and our singing group have others plans scheduled, I book various other singing groups who have joined us in making these mini-concerts most enjoyable. Another blessing is that people who have come as a result of newspaper ads, and advertisements that I have placed on bulletin boards in local supermarkets, have met up with folks whom they had not seen in over 20 years. An abundance of hugs and an overflow of love are always evident amongst guests. And more than that--God has touched hearts amazingly.

JODIE CONNECTION

For over three years after I came back to Maine in 2006, my friend Andrea and I had talked about our old friend Jodie wondering how she was and wishing that we could get together with her. To our knowledge she had resumed using her maiden name after she went through a divorce making our contacting her unattainable…or so we thought. God did not give up on our connecting with her even though we may have given up. Here is what happened (you won't believe it!):

I stopped by my son George's office one day so that he could rotate the two front tires on my car. As I sat on a chair at the expansive table in his staff meeting room, I could see out into the front office where Deb, his secretary, was standing next to one of the workers. After a brief conversation the young man headed in one direction and Deb was about to head to her desk when I hollered to her: "Who was that you were talking to, Deb?" "Micah H---", she answered. "Omgosh! Tell him to get his butt in here so that I could say hello." Come to find out, my son had hired Micah, my old friend Jodie's son, to work for him. Deb hollered out for him to come back telling him that someone wanted to see him. In walked this beautiful, young person who didn't have a clue who I was or what I wanted. "Get over here so that I could give you a kiss. I held you in my arms when you were first born," I said to Micah, "I have your picture in my photo album." Micah's parents and older sisters used to come to our house all the time in the 1970's. We were like family.

Micah was quick to pull out his wallet to show me a picture of his three year -old son who was just as cute as a button. After asking him how his different family members were doing, I told him how that Andrea and I had been wondering about his mom for years hoping to get together with her. He jotted down her phone number for me. I was blown away at how God orchestrated for my son to hire Micah in order for me and Andrea to connect with his mother whom we had been trying to locate for some time. Amazing.

A few days later I dialed the phone number. "Hi Jodie, this is B.J. "Who?" "Bette-Jean". "Bette-Jean! Oh my gosh…how are you?" The next ten minutes were filled with a whirlwind of updates of who got married and who had kids and who did this and who did that. I asked Jodie if she would like to meet me and Andrea for lunch at the cafe not too far from where she lived one day soon. "Yes", she said and we decided on a date and time. Just as we were about to hang up, Jodie, in a shy sort of way said, "I've never done anything like this before---meeting women for lunch". Gasp… Silence… Unimaginable. Jodie revealing that to me made me even more excited to get together with her. Can you imagine? I knew she was a country bumpkin, but to never have gotten together with other women for lunch not even once in her life was beyond me.

Compiling the series of events---God orchestrating Micah going to work for my son to put me, Andrea and Jodie together, and then to go beyond that and to arrange a luncheon for the three of us was the icing on the cake. He is so good! Oh, and there was yet another blessing: I had recently published one of my books of testimonies and was waiting for a shipment of books from Colorado. Oh how I prayed that the order would come before I drove all the way out to the country to Jodie's house so that I could take a copy of the book to her, so that I wouldn't have to mail it or drive all the way back there to give it to her. My prayer was answered. The book arrived the day before we went out for lunch.

The restaurant was so cozy. Maine relics were placed on shelves; newspaper clippings of historical happenings in our state were displayed here and there; checkered curtains on the windows added to the country setting. The aroma of fried seafood and other delectable foods which permeated the atmosphere whet our appetites for lunch. There were so many tempting choices on the menu we were hard pressed about what to order, although an order of French fries would have sufficed as we were more excited about filling our souls with memories than filling our tummies with good food.

Watching our old friend bask in the Father's love with us gals in the quaint country restaurant was ardently sweet to behold. And if it was sweet for us to behold, I'll just bet that all three of us were sweet for God to behold.

THE THUNDERBIRDS

In August of 2012, the Air Force Thunderbirds performed at the navy base in Brunswick, Maine. The housing complex in which I lived was situated very close by; therefore, my neighbors and I could see the air show overhead from our front yards. It was exhilarating to watch the pilots practice for two days before the big event. I was working at my computer in my bedroom the first time I heard the earsplitting boom in the sky which resounded over our houses like a train going by only amplified 100 times over. I had to drop everything and run outside as fast as I could in order to catch a glimpse of the plane as it zoomed through the sky.

Saturday was the first big performance. It was so spectacular for me to just sit in my lawn chair looking up in the sky to see the show and not to have to pay the $20.00 admission fee at the navy base. I enjoyed the attraction in the privacy of my own yard very near to my bathroom and my refrigerator.

I videoed a considerable portion of the air show although it was a tedious effort to focus on the planes as they travelled at such a high rate of speed. My favorite part of the show was when five planes flew straight up into the sky, and all the pilots simultaneously maneuvered a 180 degree turn steering their aircrafts downward - -one plane positioned in the center and the other four on the outside-- all leaving long trails of billowing exhaust behind. My neighbors and I cheered and hollered as the fete left us all breathless.

On Sunday at 8:30 a.m., I felt a forceful urge to embark on a long walk. I thought it was strange since I usually didn't walk until much later in the morning. The weather was picture perfect and I relished the cool of the morning. I walked all the way up to the main road, and turned around and headed back to my house. When I was in fairly close proximity to my house I noticed letters written in the sky. The writing gained my full attention and I immediately stopped in my tracks to read the skywriting. In humongous letters the word 'air' appeared first. I realized that it was being written by one of the thunderbird pilots. I presumed that the pilot was going to write air force. I hurried to my apartment to get my digital camera and hurried back out again. The plane, with utmost precision, maneuvered strategically to form the letter 's'. The letters 'h- o —w' followed. The pilot was announcing the air show which was to come later in the day. The pilot also drew a smiley face in the sky.

I was able to video each phase of the writing which I transferred to my computer and posted to Facebook and to You Tube for my friends who did not get to see the event. I can't tell you how many times I have watched it.

If the Holy Spirit had not urged me to take a walk that morning, I would not have seen the writing in the sky. He knew it would thrill me to see it, and therefore orchestrated changing my morning routine. It was totally exhilarating.

Thank You, God!

A SPECIAL VISIT

After I moved back to Maine from Maryland in 2006 my friend Christine from Florida e-mailed me asking if I would pay a visit (if I had a chance) to a nursing home to visit a woman who attended our church 30 years earlier. She and the woman had corresponded by mail for a substantial part of that time, but as life went on the letters became fewer and fewer until they abated altogether.

One morning the thought that I should go to visit Flossie that very day was indelible on my mind. I had called different nursing homes in an adjacent town and discovered the facility in which she was a resident. The drive there proved to be unduly problematic as the whole area had undergone a major metamorphosis since I had lived there in the 70's and 80's. None of the Mapquest directions were accurate raising my level of irritation. I resorted to pulling off the road and calling the nursing home to seek directions from one of their personnel. The staff person patiently explained the maze of roads leading to the facility. It took me at least three tries to find it.

Flossie was extremely pleasant and responsive to my greeting and small talk even though she did not remember me. She seemed to recognize my friend Christine's name when I mentioned it, even though it was obvious that she had dementia. She was as delightful as could be, a prize winning smile brightening her face. I surmised that she may not have gotten much company because she was flabbergasted that I would pay her a visit. Pure, unobtrusive Christianity oozed from the saint that lay in the bed before me. Surely, I was the one who was blessed by the visit.

While there, an intriguing thought came to mind; I would call Christine's phone number in Florida even though I knew she was at work teaching. I explained to Flossie that I would let her speak to Christine on her voicemail, although I don't think she had a clue what I meant because they didn't have voicemail in her day, but she went along with it.

Ringgg....Christine's voicemail picked up. "Christine, this is B.J. You're not going to believe where I am. I'm at the nursing home visiting Flossie. I gave her a great, big hug for you. Now I am going to put her on the phone to say hello." Undoubtedly, Flossie thought that Christine was on the phone so I had to prompt her as to what to speak into the mouthpiece like 'hello' and 'how are you' and 'I'm doing well' and so forth. She was as excited as a kid at Christmas more so because she probably hadn't used a telephone in over 20 years than anything else. It was a thrill for me to partake of her joy.

The most delightful blessing of all happened when Christine arrived home from work that day and retrieved her phone messages. She e-mailed me to express her joy at the unexpected surprise. I felt just as blessed. Who would ever think that such spontaneity and such exuberance could unfold from visiting a shut- in at a nursing home? God goes beyond our natural expectations.

GOOD FRIDAY 2012

I spent the early part of Good Friday morning 2012 reflecting on Christ's sufferings and death on the Cross, and I planned to maintain an attitude of prayer for the rest of the day. I prayed my usual morning prayers including, "You plan my day, Lord". In mid-morning my youngest son called to say that he and his girlfriend were going to bring lunch over and asked what I would like to have? Within an hour they arrived with ziti and meatballs. After we ate they insisted that they take me for a ride because it was such a beautiful, sunny day, and not only that, they wanted me to pick where I wanted to go. Wow! I was not used to surprises like that. Nor was I used to doing anything fun and exciting on a Good Friday; yet, that day was different. I believed that the Holy Spirit was planning my day. I chose to ride to the cottage that I would be renting for five days in the summer since I was warily apprehensive as to whether I would be able to locate the place or not.

The leisurely drive to Damariscotta, Maine was positively relaxing, the conversation delightfully pleasant. We drove slowly down one winding, dirt road after another passing a myriad of signs situated one on top of another identifying cottage owners. A certain stillness permeated the country roads producing inner pacification. Squirrels scrambled nearby completing the picturesque scene. The last turn-off we took was so narrow that I was certain we'd go off the road if another car came from the opposite direction. All went well, however. We arrived at our destination without any catastrophes. We spotted the campground owner in the distance standing on a ladder leaning against one of the cottages. He was most amiable and obliging, allowing us to go inside the cabin at which I would be staying to check it out even though it was off season. He was unhesitating in offering any help we might need. My son and his lady then walked down to the lake while I soaked up an inexpressible breath of fresh air while sitting in the car with the windows rolled down. I could not have been happier.

Back from the lake and into the car, my escorts got the notion to drive to Pemaquid Lighthouse. I did not know how many blessings I could handle in one day. The spontaneous events of the day were a far cry from anything I had done since my back had gotten so much worse. Off we went. We drove for 15 minutes down the road and came to the open ocean---the beautiful Atlantic Ocean--a massive stretch of blue/gray waters with waves spilling onto the sand with magical precision and a soothing motion, perfectly and exquisite like an opera or ballet. Incredible! Breathtaking! Magical! My companions walked along the shore while I hovered close to the car taking pictures and videos, pinching myself to see if it was all real, and thanking my Lord for planning the spontaneous, eventful day.

On the way back toward Route One we stopped for ice cream. I felt as if I were in seventh heaven not wanting the trip or the day to end. The blessings of the day were a reflection of God Who planned every moment. He was the One Who deserved my full attention that Good Friday; yet, He was the One Who lavished His attention on me.

BANK PERSONNEL

One morning when I was at the drive thru at my bank fairly soon after I moved to a new community, the tellers had trouble finding my account. It was understandable to me for I have a double first and a double last name; I call myself the double hyphen. After I waited for a substantial amount of time, a teller came back to the drive-up window and asked me to write down my social security number. I did so and in addition I wrote down my full legal name and my professional shortened name. When I passed the paper to her I explained that I am an author and do not use my whole legal name in publishing; I just use B.J. Peres. I asked her if she would like me to add the shortened name to my bank account. My question entered one ear and exited via the other: "You're an author! What kind of books do you write?" "Christian testimonies," I answered. By that time another teller heard me and ran to the window. The two tellers gave me 'thumbs up' signs. I gave them a 'thumbs up', as well... a nice change from the usual hum-drum banking -- such fun. It brightened my whole morning. I was awfully glad that there was no one behind me in line.

THE ROOSTER

My sister Vicki and brother-in-law Nick came to Maine for their vacation in July of 2012. They came laden with gifts. Vicki excitedly helped me to fumble through wads of newspaper to unwrap something she knew I'd go crazy over-- a ceramic rooster. She knew how much I loved to decorate my kitchen with roosters. She happened to come across the colorful spectacle at a yard sale a few weeks prior. It was brand new and still in a box. She purchased it for only $12.00; that was part of her excitement---she had made a killing.

Now, here is the rest of the story: Two years prior, my sister and I were shopping for a rooster for my kitchen at a kitchen store located in Stratford, Connecticut when I was on vacation at her house. I saw the exact same rooster that she brought to me in the store at the time, but did not want to spend $30.00 for the decorative, feathered bird so I left the store without it. I had forgotten about it, but God didn't forget.

Two years later I shrieked with excitement when I removed the wrapping from my sister's gift and saw the rooster. Two things added to my joy: the rooster matched perfectly with rooster stencils on my kitchen wall, and a bunch of grapes are built into the bottom of the rooster which match the artificial grapes I have displayed on my counter. Surely, God was behind the unexpected gift.

A WONDERFUL SURPRISE

In December of 2012 I received a Christmas card from friends who had just returned from one of the islands in the Caribbean. Tucked inside the card was a letter from a girlfriend of mine who lives on the island whom I had not seen in 13 years. I was overjoyed to receive her letter.

That evening when I had my devotional I randomly opened my Bible to the Book of Proverbs where a verse that was underlined caught my attention: "Like cold water to a thirsty soul, so is good news from a far country"…Proverbs 25:25.

MY NEW DRESS

It was a Saturday morning and I was waiting on God to see if He would lead me up the coast which is where I wanted to go or if He had other plans for me. I figured that I would meet my friend Connie in Wiscasset and give her the books she had ordered, and then head to Waldoboro to pick up my C.D.'s at Pastor Tom's church, and then head up to Rockland to visit Pastor Colby and Dottie, dear friends of mine. The first closed door was that I didn't hear from Pastor Tom by e-mail which indicated that my C.D.'s were not ready. The second closed door was that Connie's phone was busy when I tried to call her. Then I thought I'd call my prayer partner Mary to ask if she wanted to switch our prayer time and pray with me that day instead. I called her, but she already had plans. I tried calling Connie back but there was no answer; I wasn't batting very well.

I got in my car and drove to Bath, the next town over, to buy some products at one of their stores, products that I could not purchase in Brunswick. I was getting hungry and felt like having lunch with someone, anyone, but that is not what God had for me. I continued to pray for Him to lead me, to establish my steps as it says in His Word.

I drove back onto the highway and planned to get off at the Cook's Corner exit and to head home. As I drove off the exit and headed for the traffic light planning to make a right –hand turn, I felt a pull to go straight through the light. I wondered if God was leading me to drive across the street to the T.J. Maxx store (I could hear some of you now especially if you are of the male gender---'oh sure God told you to drive to T.J. Maxx--sure He did',) –but I was pretty sure He did.

Inside the store, immersed amongst racks and racks of colorful clothing, I didn't have anything in mind except to look at their clearance items which is all I ever buy when I go in there. After strolling around the store for 20 minutes or so, my eyes focused on a dress on the end of a rack right on the aisle. In the past God has always had clothing that He had picked out for me positioned on racks right on the aisle. He knew that my heart's desire for the last few years was to have a nice dress. I had resorted to skirts and tank style blouses to cover up my messed up proportions due to my back condition. Because I am exceedingly hard to fit, if I think that something looks like it was made for me, I think long and hard about not passing it by. I hemmed and hawed for a long time about the dress on the end of the rack because I did not have that kind of money to spend; it was on sale for $40.00 marked down from $118.00-- a well made garment.

I placed the dress along with a pair of slacks on sale for $7.00 in the shopping cart and headed to the fitting room to try them on. I could hardly believe that the dress actually fit me like it was made for me. I will never look great in anything, but in the dress on sale I looked as good as I would ever hope to look. I went through the mental calculations of robbing Peter to pay Paul, and decided I would make the purchase, but not without the guilty feelings that usually accompany me when I spend money even though I truly believed that God wanted me to have the pretty dress.

Two days later I had to call the power company because my online account did not make any sense to me. The woman on the other end of the line told me that it was the end of the budget season for my electricity account, and that I would not have to pay anything on my first power bill for the month of November. That meant that there would be a credit of $46.89 left over after they withdrew the payment from my bank account. My bill at the clothing store came to $49.34--that meant that the dress and slacks were gifts from God.

ELAINE'S GIFT

My girlfriend Elaine is always bringing me stuff when she travels from Massachusetts to Maine. When I was packing to move from Warren to Brunswick she showed up with the most beautiful 16"x20"gold -framed picture of an angel surrounded by an assortment of flowers. As lovely as the picture was, I thought it might be too big for my undersized, new apartment, plus I thought that the maroon matting would clash with my color schemes, but I accepted it gladly and bestowed it a home on my dinette wall. The beauty of the painting overpowered the color contrast. Once hung, every visitor to my house remarked on its beauty. An addendum to my friend's gift to me was my having to resort to using my small dinette to video my T.V. show because there was insufficient lighting to produce the show in my living room. I ended up reading my scripts from the dinette table with the beautiful painting in the background.

Thank you, Elaine.

MOTHER'S DAY 2012

After spending many a Mother's Day, Christmas and other holidays far away from my family, usually by myself or switching with other workers so that they could spend the holidays with their families, or volunteering at a hospice center, I was surprised with the most amazing Mother's Day ever eight months after I moved in close proximity to two of my sons. 'Happy Mother's Day' calls came from all my sons early in the morning, plus two friends stopped over in the late morning. In the afternoon my son Gary and daughter-in-law Brenda came to visit bringing with them my grandson David and his twins which was a total bolt out of the blue. I lay swaddled in a fleece of security.

I left at 4 o'clock to go to my son George's and daughter-in-law Sandy's for supper where my grandson Blaine and his wife, Jessica and the boys, Michael and Christopher, joined us. My great-granddaughter, Aaliyah, was there too, a combination of ages, a variety of expressions of love and caring. The day could not have been nicer. I guess for most families a Mother's Day such as this is pretty average, but to me it was extraordinary, a soul event.

MY CAMPING TRIP

I could count on one hand how many vacations I have gone on in my life mainly because some of my grandkids live in a different state than I, and through their growing up years I chose to give up my vacations to go to be with them, or to have them come to my house during their school vacations. Finances have been a factor most of the time, as well, and much later in life my disability from a bad back has prevented me from doing any lengthy traveling. Plus, living on social security presents limitations of its own, to be sure.

In the summer of 2011, I went with my girlfriend Elaine to a Christian campsite in Damariscotta, Maine where some members of my friend

Pastor Tom's church own a lovely campground on a beautiful lake. I learned that they rented out their cabins to Christians and did not charge a specific amount of money for them, but just asked for an offering-- whatever 'would be' campers could afford. Did I hear that right? I was dumbfounded! I did not have to take the time to mull it around in my mind. Since I could never afford to go anywhere, it had to be God's provision for me to get away. I tucked the info in the back of my mind.

The following February I read a post on Facebook written by my friend, Pastor Tom, reminding all of his church members and friends to reserve their cottages early before they were all rented out. Had he not written the reminder, there is no way I would have remembered to do it. I immediately contacted the campground owners and reserved a cottage for three days. When I mentioned the reservation to Pastor Tom, pointing out that I truly wanted to stay longer, but couldn't because of the lack of funds, he prompted me to call the campground owners back and to request an additional two days explaining to me that they would not want money to restrict me to a three day stay. I followed his suggestion.

I planned the five-day trip with great anticipation. A vacation on a lake would be such a monumental happening for me as my life consisted mainly of writing, writing and more writing. Worries about how I would manage to carry all the camping supplies hovered in the back of my mind; however, I kept them in prayer and would not let myself waver. I could not allow anything to prevent me from undertaking an opportunity of a lifetime.

The day of my anticipated getaway arrived toward the end of July in 2012. I left my house early in the morning and took a leisurely ride up the coast. I was bursting with adventure. How amazing to realize how much good a sunny day with no commitments or responsibilities can do for a soul. I had traveled Route One extensively over the years, yet each trip was to fulfill an appointment on my calendar or to visit family. I had never had the luxury of traveling the sometimes monotonous highway at my leisure. The mental freedom allowed me to stop to browse in stores whenever I felt like it. What a feeling not to be pressed for time! That part of the trip was a vacation in itself.

Having driven to the campground beforehand with my son, I had the directions down pat; there was no guess work or getting lost. Because of the lack of pressure and distractions, my senses were magnificently heightened and I was able to behold nature like never before. The smell from the mudflats at low tide from the many waterways which dotted the coastline was more prominent than usual. Noisy seagulls zoomed to the flats to scoop up worms to swallow, and clams to hold tightly in their bills while making an ascent of several feet into the air and then dropping the clams onto the rocks below to cause them to shatter and break, then racing back down to the rocks to claim their catch and to eat the delicacies.

After accomplishing the difficult task of unloading the car and settling into the cottage, I got comfortable on my chaise lounge on the screened-in porch taking in the bustling sounds of the squirrels, birds, acorns falling from huge oaks and hitting the roof tops, the waving hands of camping neighbors and a holy stillness in the air. Although I had brought plenty of reading material with me, there was a big selection of inspirational books and videos in the cottage for all campers. I began to read one of those books. Later in the morning the campground owners said that I didn't have to walk the long distance to the lake with my cane, but that I could drive my car down. I gladly accepted their offer and did just that. The lake was calling my name. I wasted no time getting wet with one of the floating devices housed in a screen house on the water's edge. I frolicked like a happy puppy in the water jumping waves from passing boats. When I grew tired I put my chaise lounge inside the screen-house at the water's edge and lay back to read. I was certain that no one on the face of the earth who had spent a few thousand dollars on a vacation could experience the peace and relaxation that I felt at that very moment and for only a small fraction of their cost.

That evening I met my next door camping neighbors and their two small children. What an absolute joy to observe the way they were raising their kids. There was no comparison to the average parent/children household. Truly, the family was refreshing to me. I actually went to sleep with the cottage door open as I love the fresh air and the cold. A small hook lock on the screen door could not ward off a child let alone a robber but that did not matter to me; my only thoughts were of the solitude.

The following day I drove into the quaint town of Damariscotta to pick up a few items at a local market. The morning after that I drove to Rockland to visit my friends Pastor Colby and his wife Dottie. From there I met up with a former prison inmate whom I used to visit when I was involved in prison ministry. He, his girlfriend and I, had lunch at a popular, local Chinese restaurant. On the way back to the campground I stopped to visit a woman in her nineties whom I had not seen in two years. She lived in a boarding home in the Town of Thomaston. Boy was she surprised to see me! On Saturday morning I drove to my friend Norma's in a nearby town. My former neighbors Karen and Marie and Marie's grandson, Kyle, came to the cottage to visit me in the afternoon. We walked down to the lake where Kyle and I went swimming. We followed our swim with a nice lunch.

On Saturday night, the Kinney's, more camping neighbors, drove me to a barbeque and concert at the church I used to attend in Searsmont, Maine. They knew how much I wanted to attend so that I could see my former church family, but that I was leery about driving on the dark roads by myself. What a wonderful gesture on their part.

Sunday morning: Church service in the screened area; Sunday afternoon: Another concert … 'Could this be wonderland,' I asked myself, 'or was it a little bit of heaven on earth?'

On Monday morning the Kinney's and I boarded a pontoon boat operated by the campground owner. He and his wife had prepared a delicious breakfast for us including egg and sausage sandwiches and freshly baked cinnamon coffee cake; the smell was tantalizing. They navigated the pontoon to a cove, a far reaching distance from the campground. Loons flew about noisily as if to bid good morning to the other creatures of nature. Tranquility encompassed us; stillness enraptured us. For two hours we enjoyed eating, sharing stories about our Christian lives and sitting quietly and motionless as we sat at the Master's banqueting table with His banner of love hovering over us. At that moment it was as if even the turquoise waters of the Caribbean where I had basked in the sun on private beaches years earlier could not afford more serenity than what surrounded us on the still waters in the hidden cove on the lake that glorious morning.

All good things must come to an end and so it was with our morning excursion. Maynard started the engine as Sandra collected the breakfast leftovers and we headed back to the campground. Did it have to end? I wondered. I wanted that captivating feeling to last forever. The voices of campers came into earshot as we got closer to the pier. In another few seconds my wonderful five -day vacation would come to an end. I would take the thoughts of my vacation home with me and reminisce for a long time afterward.

My camping neighbors Steve and Rhonda Kinney and I have kept in touch via Facebook, as well as the camp owners Sandra and Maynard and other camping neighbors Leigh and Nate. Rhonda even came to visit me one Saturday, and she and Steve came to visit me together one time. They will be camping near me in 2014. These are God-ordained friendships, to be sure.

Needless to say, there is no way that I could have planned a get-away like the one in Damariscotta on my own. It was important to God that I get away. I couldn't afford much; He knew that. He orchestrated the whole trip and blessed me beyond what I could have ever dreamed.

Six weeks later in September of 2012, I rented a different cottage on the campground for two days. Again, my stay was positively delightful. Steve and Rhonda returned to the campground at the same time, and we again enjoyed one another's company. I met additional new friends, plus another one of my girlfriends drove to the lake to spend time with me. That Saturday evening there was an awesome concert in the screen house after which Steve and Rhonda invited me to sit around their campfire with them. We enjoyed sweet fellowship as the melodious sounds from the crackling wood completed the tranquil atmosphere--another blessed time from God.

A BLESSING FROM MY FRIEND

I interviewed my friend, Pastor Larry, for my T.V. show spontaneously at a Denny's Restaurant when he visited Maine in October 2011. We had gotten together to discuss a documentary which he considered undertaking. He wondered if I would get on board at the onset of the project by conducting some interviews for him in my neck of the woods. After we ate and discussed the plans, I asked him unhesitatingly if I could interview him for my T.V. show. "Sure", he replied. I had nothing on which to raise my camera up higher than the table so I made a make-shift tri-pod with a napkin holder, salt and pepper shakers and even a butter knife. Whatever worked…

A few months later I received an e-mail from my friend, Pastor Larry:

Hi B.J.-- 2012 --Greetings in the Lord - I trust you had a blessed Christmas & New Year season. We are surely looking forward to a glorious 2012 in the plan and purpose of our precious Lord.

I'd like to share a couple of things with you.

Firstly, you will be quite amazed to know that I received a stunning email literally a WEEK after we did the interview - from the most unlikely source. It was from the girl I took to our Senior Prom!!!! No kidding. She had eventually found me on Facebook 2 years ago, and we traded a couple of friendly emails. She lives out in AZ with her family and was trying to find old friends.

This latest email was because she was actually doing research about Europe (I believe...) in you tube and came across our video interview. Is that amazing, or what??? She was quite blessed and expressed a spiritual appreciation for what we talked about.

blessings in the Lord, p la

(The video he referred to was the one he and I did at Denny's Restaurant).

I don't care what kind of T.V. program that Hollywood could come up with, nobody can outdo the ingenious, original, inspiring stories with which God blesses us.

THE WALKER

My doctor filled out a paper to have Medicare pay for a fold -up walker for me, one that I could store in the trunk of my car and to which I could have easy access. I took the necessary papers which I had my primary care physician sign, to a local medical supply company where one of the employees spent a whole hour measuring me and having me try out a small walker to fit my small frame. After an hour we sat down to fill out the necessary paper work for Medicare. One of the questions the employee asked me was if I needed to use the walker to get around my house. "No. I get around my apartment without a walker; I just need one to carry on the bus with me when I go downtown." The woman then proceeded to tell me that Medicare would not pay for a walker unless the walker was necessary for the applicant to walk around his/her house.

I thanked her for all the time she spent with me, and told her that I would have to start saving money to buy the walker on my own which would take quite a while. Feeling sad for me, she indirectly tried to coerce me to make things simple by having her write down the word 'yes' in the allotted space on the paper stating that I indeed needed a walker to use in my house.

In my estimation lying on the Medicare papers would be like stealing from the United Sates government, and in doing so, I would, in fact, be stealing from my neighbors. And even more than that, it would be lying before God. There was no way…

The following day I was headed to do my laundry in the clubhouse across the street from my apartment, but the Holy Spirit said to wait until the following day to do the laundry, so I went over early on the second morning. A bunch of us women were chatting in the laundry area when one of the maintenance men came in to tell us that there was a large number of walkers and other medical supplies donated to the complex that were upstairs in the storage area. He was going to bring them all downstairs, and anyone who needed anything could take whatever they needed free of charge. My friend Ellie said that she had a fold up walker that she wanted to trade for one with a seat. It was a small walker and a perfect fit for me and so they gave it to me.

I truly believe that God was honoring me for not obtaining the walker fraudulently at the medical supply company. And furthermore, if I had gone to the Laundromat when I wanted to go, and not when God told me to go, I would have missed out on all the equipment being given away. God had all the bases covered.

BLOWN AWAY

After reconnecting with an old acquaintance, Gloria, from 50 years earlier on Facebook in 2011, and after becoming closely knitted together with her in Jesus Christ for one year, I nonchalantly mentioned to her one day that I received Christ into my heart as my Savior in April 1971. Her next words to me were: "I asked Christ into my heart in April 1971". "What!!" "Yes, I was saved in April 1971". She was saved the same month and year as me. That was no small potatoes, no coincidence. God not only reconnected us, He initiated that conversation after a year had gone by. Just imagine-- He called us both into His kingdom at the same time 40 years prior. What a blessing!

ASK AND KEEP ON ASKING

My former prayer partner, Mary, from Midcoast Maine and I prayed in her town down at the river every other Tuesday for as long as I lived in Brunswick. I don't know why we were led to go to the water's edge, to park the car and to pray with seagulls perching on rocks around us and occasional logs of wood rushing down the river passed us, yet we were pulled there as if being vacuumed.

One morning during our prayer time whereby we petitioned God for everything under the sun, and for blessings for just about everyone under the sun, I felt the urge to pray for a special blessing for Mary and for myself that very day. I left the requests at God's altar. An hour later I started the car and headed for Mary's house to drop her off. She brought me out two, homemade whoopie pies that her daughter, Denise, had made the night before. My mouth was drooling for a bite; they were the real deal.

By evening I had forgotten about having asked for a special blessing for myself that day until I got on Facebook and noticed a 'like' on one of my posts having to do with the small things in life being the biggest. What blessed me was that one of the people who liked my post was a former employer of mine whom I always felt looked down on me. I could not imagine him liking anything I posted no matter how inspirational it was. I do not believe that the person would have made the effort to comment had it not been for my specific prayer for a blessing that morning. God does not take our prayers lightly no matter how small or insignificant we think they may be. Each prayer bombards heaven and allows God to bless us.

CHAPTER 2

GOD'S ORCHESTRATION

JESUS

One day when Jesus went to the synagogue it was His turn to read from the Scriptures. The Torah was opened to the page on which the decorative bookmark was placed. He stood up to read, "These words are fulfilled". He was reading from Isaiah's prophecy of Himself. Just picture the Son of God standing in the front of the synagogue facing the Jewish members. Not only did He read the words, but spoke them in the present tense referring to Himself. So intense! What were the odds of Him being called to begin reading in the exact place of His death being prophesied? That was divine orchestration by God, the Holy Spirit.

That type of orchestration is precisely the same type of orchestration which God has used globally for centuries and continues to use, and shall continue to use in our lives until He comes in the rapture. Every divine appointment we have is an orchestration of God.

NINE MONTHS OVER-DO

After doing my laundry one morning I was tired and didn't want to go anyplace else, but the thought kept coming to me that I should call the library to have them reserve a book for me. That seemed somewhat bizarre because I had already borrowed three books from the lending library in my complex that morning; yet, I acted on it. I made the call and was instructed to leave my phone number. A librarian called back within reasonable time to say that they were holding the book I reserved, and that I could pick it up anytime.

Another thought came to mind-- that I should go to the farmer's market at the mall. I didn't know how I would handle the walking because of my back pain, but the thought echoed in my mind. I have learned over the years that it is not a good idea to disregard thoughts that keep coming to us.

I picked up the book I had reserved at the library and headed for the mall. Oh brother! The summer people were in town in full force--on the mall, in the streets and all over the place. Young guys and gals walked a variety of dogs on leashes. Moms and grandmothers pushed baby strollers while toddlers chased balls. The lobster ladies waited on swarms of customers in front of their stand. Seniors sat on park benches alongside workers who were eating hot dogs, hamburgers and French fries during their lunch break. Bicyclists rode on a path through the grassy mall and on the outskirts. Motorcyclists with bandana's across their brows and their girlfriends behind them with their arms wrapped around their torsos whizzed by circling the mall.

The usual amount of downtown traffic at noon was dreadful enough, but with the increased traffic it was bedlam. Nobody would even let me cross over one lane of traffic to park diagonally alongside the mall. I kept driving slowly with my left blinker on; yet, to my disillusionment my predicament escalated. I wondered how I had survived driving on the Baltimore Beltway for so many years. I was starting to lose it because I was slowing down traffic behind me. Then, suddenly, a car stopped and the courteous driver let me drive in front of him into a parking place right in front of a taco lunch wagon.

As I got out of my car and locked the door, a man from inside the lunch wagon who was leaning against one end of the eatery as he observed walkers and traffic called out to me. "Your inspection sticker ran out last August—2011". Yikes! It was May 25, 2012! "For some reason I was thinking I had until August 2012 to get my car inspected," I hollered to the man. "You are lucky you haven't been stopped by a policeman," he said. I could not thank him enough. I immediately called my son who got right on it, and arranged with his mechanic to get me in for an appointment for an inspection right away.

God orchestrated my goings and my comings that morning. I gave Him my day and asked Him to lead me in whatever He wanted me to do; He certainly did. The Holy Spirit is the One Who kept prompting me to go downtown. He is the One, Who, through His ministering angels, would not allow any drivers to give me the courtesy of turning into a parking place until I was precisely at the place where God wanted me to park. He also arranged that there would be no customers at the time I parked in front of the taco lunch wagon, in order that the worker would not be waiting on customers, but would be standing against the side of the building watching people and cars when I pulled up.

Thank You, Lord. You spared me from getting a hefty fine. You are so faithful.

(I hope that my readers will not do what some of my friends did when I related this happening to them and fail to see God in it. They reasoned that if God were in it He would not have waited nine months to call it to my attention. THEY MISSED THE POINT! The point was that God prevented me from getting a heavy fine. The longer we go passed the expiration date on details like that, the more incredible the testimony. They also missed the point of the impeccable precision and timing orchestrated by God to lead me to park in that precise parking place.

ANDREW'S BIRTHDAY

For some reason when I was writing down all the September birthdays on my shopping list one year, I forgot to write down my great-grandson Andrew's birthday. I had purchased all my monthly birthday cards, and went through all of them placing tiny sticky notes on each one reminding me when to mail them. Ten days after that it came to my attention that Andrew was having a birthday in September. Oh no, I thought. My car was broke down and I couldn't get to the store to buy him a card. I sent cards to his brother and all his cousins. I did not want him to feel slighted because he didn't receive one.

On Andrew's actually birthday I sent him a birthday wish on Facebook along with posting an Alvin and the Chipmunk's birthday song at his Facebook site. As soon as I got brake pads put on my car I went to town to get groceries. As I walked down the aisles of the supermarket I came across a woman pushing her little grandson in a grocery cart. "He looks like such a nice little boy", I said. "Oh, he is", she responded. "What's your name, honey", I asked. "Drew", he replied.

Drew being short for Andrew, I immediate realized that God was reminding me to pick up a birthday card for my great-grandson Andrew which I had forgotten all about.

If I had driven all the way home and then realized that I had forgotten to purchase the birthday card, I would have been very upset because there are no stores around where I live that sell cards. God is everything to me--not only the Creator and the Designer of the universe, my Healer, Soul Mate, Friend, Counselor, Confidant, and more; He reminds me of the things I forget. How I praise Him!

JUST A STROLL

My next door neighbor and I were taking a stroll one summer afternoon and stopped to visit a lady named Hilda. She and I had a mutual friend, Arline, from northern Maine. I mentioned to Hilda that I left a message on Arline's voicemail and was waiting to get a call back. Without hesitation she replied, "You won't be getting a call back because Arline is in the hospital; she fell and broke her hip". "What?" Hilda proceeded to tell me the details of Arline's injury and that she was in the hospital.

The amazing part of this story is that when my neighbor and I took walks we never crossed the street; yet, on that particular day I said to her, "Let's cross the street and go and say hi to those women over there". Had I not done that I would not have known about Arline's accident, and would have wondered why I didn't receive a call back. All three of us were blown away by God's orchestration.

MY SISTER'S STORY

My sister, Vicki, called one day to tell me what had happened when she and my brother-in-law, Nick, left a Costco store in Connecticut and walked to their car in the parking lot. Three grocery carts were near their car. One of the carts had a grocery bag in it which revealed a large container of coffee. Vicki wanted to take it home and to save it for me because it wasn't the kind they used. Nick protested saying that someone may have tampered with it. She examined it and said that no one tampered with it. She reasoned that if she took the coffee back in the store that it would be put back on the shelf. She did not want that to happen after someone had paid for it, so she took the coffee home to put away for me or someone else who could use it.

That night the couple congregated with their neighbors at the clubhouse in their gated community. Their friend, Barbara, told the ladies about how upset she was because she left a big tin of coffee that she bought that morning at Costco in a grocery cart in the parking lot. She said that she even called the store to see if anyone found it. Vicki was dumbfounded and could hardly get the words out fast enough, "Barbara, you're not going to believe this, but I have your coffee". "What!" Barbara blurted out. Vicki proceeded to relate to Barbara and the ladies everything that had happened that morning. Nobody could believe it.

My sister could not wait to call me to tell me about it because she knows that I attribute these happenings to God. She was right because I do think that God was behind that incident. If only they all knew that we Christians in the Body of Christ experience these neat happenings ongoing. This is why we are so filled with the joy of the Lord all of the time.

AT A FUNERAL PARLOR NO LESS

My sister, Vicki, called me one day to tell me that she went to a funeral parlor a couple of days prior to pay her respects to someone who had passed away. After a short stay she headed toward the exit when she ran into an old acquaintance from the neighborhood where we grew up. It turned out that the acquaintance, Beverly, had gone to the wrong funeral parlor by mistake.

Well, it was no mistake in God's eyes. He is the One Who orchestrated that to happen wanting the ladies from the old neighborhood to cross paths. Don't you just love it!

MY FAVORITE T.V. SHOW

My favorite T.V. show used to be, 'Who Do You Think You Are', which featured someone famous tracing his/her genealogy with the help of experts. It was always so exciting to see the different reactions of people when they found out who their ancestors were. The show used to air on Friday nights.

One Friday I had company for supper and afterward we enjoyed Christian fellowship. It was in the back of my mind that I would miss one of only a few shows I watched on T.V. during the week, but it did not matter. I enjoyed entertaining company much more than watching a show on genealogy. Beep-beep-beep…"What's that noise coming from the bedroom?" my friend asked. "Oh, that's just my alarm clock", I responded. I always set it for 8 o'clock on Friday nights. I proceeded to tell her about the popular show of which she had never heard. She expressed an interest in checking it out sometime. I assured her that a re-run more than likely would be shown that night and there was no need for me to watch it.

Ten minutes later my guest thought she would get ready to leave as she had an hour drive ahead of her. We exchanged goodbyes and I turned on the T.V. guessing that the aired segment would be a re-run. Not so. The segment featured Reba McIntyre and I had not seen it before. I sat back and thoroughly enjoyed it.

The point of this story is that I put God first in having one of the Lord's people visit my home. I wasn't up to having company; yet, I put God first. God, in turn, enabled me to watch my favorite show. I was blessed.

Here is another testimony regarding the same T.V. show:

I had been sleeping on my air mattress on the living room floor for eight months due to noise in the apartment building adjacent to my bedroom during the night. One night, however, I felt like sleeping in my bed for a change because I desperately missed its comfort. Strangely, the Holy Spirit prompted me to sleep in the living room again. I obeyed without questioning Him. Well, what do you suppose? It was a Friday night, and, as usual, when sleeping on the floor I turned on the T.V and set the sleep alarm on the remote control. I made myself comfortable and waited to see what show would air. The music sounded familiar. I could not believe my ears. The title of the show appeared across the screen 'Who Do You Think You Are?'…my favorite T.V. show. I could not believe my eyes. I discovered that I had it written on my calendar, but had forgotten to check it. God even had that oversight covered; it was one of His nuggets. He knew that if I had missed it I would have been unhappy so He planned for me to see it.

GOD SAVED THE MEATLOAF

I had a small meatloaf in the oven and turned it on low to 275 degrees thinking that I would let it bake slowly for a few hours. I did not set my alarm clock as I usually do when cooking food in the oven figuring all would be well at such a low temperature; but, I got busy and forgot about it. God, Who always intervenes in my life no matter how trivial something may seem, caused something to occur so that my meatloaf would not burn to a crisp. After never losing power in the year that I lived in Brunswick at the time, I lost power that afternoon for three to four hours. When I finally remembered that I had a meatloaf in the oven and opened the oven door, I discovered that it was cooked perfectly. Had the power not gone out, it would have burnt to smithereens after being in the oven for all those hours. Thank You, Lord.

THE DETERGENT

Ordinarily, I go to the Laundromat around 9 o'clock in the morning, but one day I distinctly heard the Holy Spirit tell me to go at 7 o'clock instead so off I went at the crack of dawn. I loaded a big, front loader with clothes, and instead of pouring in the laundry detergent from the bottle without measuring the way I normally do, I poured a very small amount into the cap and then poured it in the compartment on top of the machine. Next, I turned the knob to cotton/hot and put eight quarters into the slot. I went to sit down on a comfortable recliner provided for the residents of the complex. Aside from the roar of the washers and the tumbling of the dryers, the recliners provided maximum rest and relaxation. I think I was the only resident that took full advantage of them and laid all the way back on them.

I couldn't relax as I had anticipated that morning for I began to wonder if I had put enough detergent into the compartment. I wondered if I might have put in only an eighth of a cup of detergent rather than a quarter of a cup. As I was thinking those thoughts, a woman whom I knew by sight called to me, "Oh dear--I put my detergent into your machine by mistake instead of putting it into mine which is right next to yours. I am so sorry". She was so embarrassed.

"Oh, it's not a problem," I hollered to her, "I didn't think I put in enough detergent anyway".

Coincidence? Positively, absolutely not! God is with me wherever I go, watching whatever I do, and He honestly does help me all the time even when I need a little extra laundry detergent.

THE 2,000 PIECE PUZZLE

Amongst presents that my son Gary and daughter-in-law Brenda gave me one Christmas was a 2,000 piece puzzle of the Last Supper. I started putting it together right after the New Year. The biggest percentages of the pieces were black so working on it was murder. After placing roughly 1900 pieces into the designated places, I came to a temporary dead end. The dead end caused me to lose my enthusiasm to work on the puzzle. God used that time to tug at my heart about being addicted to puzzles. I had an excuse ready for Him. I tooted my own horn while I played my imaginary violin as I reminded God how that I always did my Christian work first before I played. My words seemed to fall on deaf ears because I could still hear the still, small voice of the Holy Spirit telling me what a waste of time a 2,000 piece puzzle was especially when it had nothing to do with eternity.

Within minutes I put a disk into the C.D. player. It was of a class taught by my founding pastor on Psalm Two. Within the first five minutes of the message, God spoke to me as my pastor posed this question and these statements: 'What is my full potential?' 'Give up what you need to give up'. 'Work hard and work smart to accomplish it'.

My self analysis: What was my full potential? My full potential was to get on more T.V. stations for Him; however, I was comfortable with the 10 stations I already had, and really didn't want to take on any more work or any more expenses.

God: Those are projections.

Me:: What do I need to give up?

God: The puzzle.

I immediately knew the answer in my spirit. Here is the sweet part of the communication: God did not give me this message while I was working on the puzzle. He waited until after I covered the puzzle with a tablecloth with no plans to finish it to let me know His thoughts. Truly, that was grace personified.

I tuned my ears to listen to the rest of the compelling C.D. My pastor went on to teach that we should dream success for God and it will come to pass. Don't you just love that! In other words: I should dream of a successful T.V. show with many more stations for God, even stations in big cities, and it will come to pass. Work hard and work smart to accomplish it meant exactly that--all those hours I put into the puzzle I could have utilized by promoting my show which could potentially reach thousands of viewers with the gospel. We are living in the end times and as souls are going to hell all the hundreds of hours that I was wasting on a puzzle were for naught.

If you are a puzzle maker please do not be introspective as you read this. Doing puzzles is not sin; it is a hobby that is fun and relaxing and also helps to stimulate our minds. My testimony about being led to give up puzzles has to do with God's calling on my life. I was spending too much of His time on things that were not eternal. It is no different than being a college student and having the professor telling his students that they cannot use their cell phones nor do puzzles in class. I am in God's college and I am here to learn. He allows me plenty of time for movies and relaxing; yet, He has to remind me that He expects more of my time. I should give Him all my time after all He has done for me.

SECOND PART OF THE PUZZLE TESTIMONY

Even before I had placed a tablecloth over the huge puzzle I had been working on and placed a centerpiece in the middle of the tablecloth, I could see that there was a piece missing. I searched high and low for it, unsuccessfully, for weeks. I was just plain tired of working on the puzzle, and after hearing from God about His thoughts on it, I needed to digest His words. I made a deliberate decision to finish my puzzle project, to glue it and to give it away and then to replace my puzzle time with more writing. I removed the tablecloth from the dinette table. Then I glued the top side of the puzzle and allowed it to dry. The following day I turned it around as awkward a job as it was. I had planned to fashion a make-do puzzle piece to fill in the space where the puzzle piece was missing. I had done that sort of thing many times before using a pen to mark the outline of the piece and coloring in the inside with crayon. It never came out perfectly, yet it always appeared moderately camouflaged.

I had placed two large sheets of poster paper which I had stapled together underneath the puzzle as I worked on it. I was very careful as I removed the posters from beneath the puzzle so that I could turn it over to glue the bottom side of it. As I performed the maneuver my head happened to be turned toward the right for a fleeting second, whereupon I happened to see a small speck on the floor in the peripheral vision of my right eye. 'I just cleaned this floor,' I said to myself, 'what on earth could that be?' Closer investigation revealed that the small object was, in fact, the missing 2,000th piece of the puzzle which had been missing for a few months. There was no longer any reason for me to improvise with a fake puzzle piece; the puzzle was whole. What a thrill! I could hardly contain myself. I had to tell my family members and friends because they all knew about the missing puzzle piece.

My perspective on the way things unfolded was that God orchestrated my receiving a message from Him through working on the puzzle, and ultimately orchestrated my finding the puzzle piece after I responded to His message given to me through the C.D. of Psalm Two. Yes, you're reading this correctly. If I had not responded to His message, I may not have found the missing puzzle piece. Response to Him always brings blessings.

GOD CHANGED MY APPOINTMENTS

It was on my schedule one Tuesday morning to pick up my friend, Mary, in Bath for a Revelations class at my house. My friend, Val, was supposed to come to the class after which she would take Mary home as I had a doctor's appointment for a bone density test in Brunswick at 2 o'clock that afternoon. Concurrent with all that was going on, I had a problem with my eye which had taken a turn for the worse that day; the lower eyelid was swollen. I had discovered the swelling while examining my eye closely in the car mirror in the daylight. I also discovered a pus - filled pore that was pink and inflamed. An annoying sensation made my eye feel as if something was inside it. My vision was blurred and accompanied with minimal pain. I called the eye doctor to see if they could squeeze me in that morning rather than to wait for my previously scheduled eye appointment for the following Monday.

As I drove along the highway on the way to Mary's house my phone rang. The screening department at the medical center had called to inform me that their person who performed the bone density tests did not show up for work that day so they had to postpone my appointment; they were apologetic…Zippadee-doo-dah! I was glad that the tech had not shown up for work. It was obvious that God was in action--oh, how I knew that I knew!

After arriving back at my house with Mary and putting the Book of Revelations D.V.D. in the player for her, I called the eye doctor. Get this--they had a 1:30 p.m. slot open, but it was for their Bath office, not their Brunswick office where I lived. But--- since my friend, Val, never showed up for the class (I think her daughter-in-law went into labor,) I would have to take Mary home to Bath anyway, so it all worked out. The eye doctor's Bath office was down the street from Mary's house. And since we would have an hour and a half in between the class, our prayer time and my appointment, she joined me at the Irish pub restaurant in her town where we enjoyed a delightful lunch on one of my Christmas gift certificates. Could things get any smoother!

I made it to the eye doctor's in plenty of time, and it turned out that my eye condition was not serious. It did not require any medicine just daily hot compresses for several weeks. I just love it when God displays His uniqueness and His diversified orchestrations. Everything that we plan and everything that we do should be tentative. All we need to do is to keep our eyes and ears open to Him and to go along for the ride…..amen?

THE WRAPPER

This definitely isn't a 4th of July fireworks testimony, yet that fact does not trivialize it at all.

My friend Rhonda drove to Topsham, the town next to Brunswick, with a friend one Saturday, and I met her there and drove her back to my place. She brought with her a container of soup for our lunch. I baked some refrigerated biscuits to go with the soup. Because she was on a strict diet for her health, she asked if I had the wrapper for the biscuits so that she could read the list of ingredients. It just so happened that for the first time ever, I saved the wrapper and put it in a small plastic bag with the remainder of the biscuits back in the refrigerator….unbelievable!!!!

COUSIN THOMAS

One night when I was not tired enough to sleep, I considered watching a movie on my computer to help me doze off. The Lord spoke to me and said to conduct my quarterly search on Facebook to try to locate people from my past along with distant relatives instead of watching a movie.

So there I was in my p j's racking my brain for names of people with whom I used to go to school; names of my second and third cousins; even names of people in Italy with the same names as my deceased grandparents. Usually I find myself reading information and viewing photos, but not that night. That night I was only successful in finding the Facebook site for one person on my list: a young man who used to be my son Gary's best friend in grade school. I had never stopped praying for him all through the years. I decided to drop him a note. Faces and posts on Facebook began to meld into one another making me weary. Peoples' posts airing their woes started to pull me down.

Tiredness and boredom were on the threshold of overpowering me. I was ready to turn off the computer--but suddenly—astonishingly--my hands wouldn't allow me to perform the simple function of shutting down the monitor and hard drive. Simultaneously, God said in His still, small voice not to abandon my searches. I knew from the ways He had prodded at me all my life that I was not supposed to succumb to my tiredness or boredom; I was to continue searching. But for whom was I supposed to search? I wondered. Mentally I went through a list of all 33 cousins on my father's side and all their kids. My second cousin, Thomas, came to mind. He was my Cousin Larry's son. His whole family lived in California.

Thomas and I used to be Facebook friends when Facebook was first introduced four or five years prior. About a year after that, however, he dropped me from his friend's list assumedly because of all the spiritual stuff I had on my page, and assumedly because of the fact that he was a party boy and had a great deal of questionable posts at his site; I was not at all slighted.

When I typed in Thomas' name in the search bar, I almost fell off my desk chair at what came up on the screen--Thomas' obituary! There was no mistake. I clicked on the obituary and all my family members were listed. He passed away in August, two months prior, at the age of 42. My heart nearly stopped. My youngest son was the exact same age; it more than hit home. I had never met my second cousin in person because of the many miles between us geographically, yet the same blood flowed through our veins. And to think that I wanted to get off the computer and that God would not let my hands function until He got His message across to me to keep searching!

Thomas' dad, my cousin Larry, was a very tender -hearted man. I remembered when his dad (my uncle) passed away, and we spent time on the phone and I would hear him crying. This was a grown man, an elected official and a leader in his community. If he had that difficult of a time in losing his dad, how terrible had it been for him to have lost his son? I wished I could have been there for him in his time of grief, if not in person at least over the phone.

I was awake for hours. I was so wound up that I could not sleep. I could not for the life of me figure out how that information had not reached me in two months. I had a tremendous urge to call my cousin, at least to write to him to express my condolences, but I had to wait to see if God would lead. The following day I found out from an aunt of mine certain circumstances regarding the death, and it was important that I respect my cousin's wishes to keep the matter private due to the nature of his son's passing (very difficult for me).

As sad as it was to learn about Thomas' passing, I was in awe at how specifically God had orchestrated the whole event of my learning the news. Just one day earlier I had meditated on how impossible it was to keep up with correspondence and updates with several hundred family members and friends and with my work schedule; yet, God in His faithfulness has never failed to put people on my mind, or to remind me of things that I am supposed to do. He never misses anything. Makes me want to fall on my face and to venerate Him.

SHE NEVER CALLED

I was waiting for a call from a friend from Vermont, who with her husband and another couple, were on their way north to Maine. We were supposed to have lunch together in my town. I was doing an errand while waiting for the call to come through. I was in my car waiting for a red light to turn green on the way to the WalMart to pick up a site- to -store order when my cell phone rang. It was a pastor friend of mine calling from another city in Maine to tell me that our mutual out-of-state friends were in his area at the cottage they had rented. I said, "What! We're supposed to have lunch together. I have been waiting for them to ride through Brunswick and to call me. It's a good thing you called me, pastor. My day would have been ruined if I sat around waiting and waiting. Thank you so much." God did it again.

I'm certain that my friend got busy packing the car for the trip and tending to last minute details; I have never mentioned it to her. I call it the goodness of God that prevented me from wasting a lot of time. It is the easiest thing in the world to brush off these things as happenstance—yet—they are not happenstance at all. God is behind all of them.

RIGHT TO THE DOLLAR

One Sunday after church I drove out of the church parking lot as usual with thoughts of dinner on my mind. After hemming and hawing about whether I should spend money at a restaurant or wait until I arrived home to eat, and after my tummy won out, I decided to look for an Olive Garden Restaurant in South Portland, Maine on the way back to Brunswick; I just love the food there; that is where I ended up. As soon as I glanced at the menu I realized that the prices were higher than at their sister restaurant I had dined at in another city. I was seated comfortably and did not want to leave to go someplace cheaper so I placed an order. As I sat in the booth admiring the lovely display of colorful pieces- many with an Italian theme- I couldn't help but over-hear the conversation from the three women sitting in the next booth. They were manifesting their love for God and sharing testimonies not caring who heard them. They were unquestionably delightful to over-hear.

The meal was positively delectable. I savored every mouthful before packing what I could not eat into a doggie box to take home with me. The waitress delivered the check which totaled $14.45. I divulged to her that their prices were higher than at the other Olive Garden. "Oh no; they're all the same", she replied. "Well, this same meal only cost me $9.90 at the other restaurant". "The reason you are paying more is because you ordered from the dinner menu. You must have gotten the lunch portion at the other place". "Oh, yes, you are right. I did get a lunch portion. But, why didn't you give me a lunch menu?" "You have to ask for one, she said". …Live and learn.

I added a 20 percent tip, paid the bill and exited, chalking it up to experience. On the way out I paused at the next booth and mentioned to the three women patrons that their conversation about God in public was very refreshing to me. It was so much nicer than hearing swear words and discussions about family problems and such. The three women bid me God's blessings.

As I started down the highway I kept punishing myself for spending that much money on a noonday meal as I have such a small appetite. I chided myself knowing that I could only afford a small number of luncheons throughout the month as I am on a fixed income. I tried to push the condemning thoughts away dozens of times through the day; yet, they resurfaced all that night and into the next day.

On Monday I went to take out the garbage and there were two papers stuck in my door from the office in my complex. One paper stated that the tenants' utility allowance went up seven dollars for the months of June and July. The other paper had written on it that we tenants should pick up our refund checks at the office on Friday.

The amount of my refund was to be $14.00. I was dumbfounded! The refund would cover the $14.45 that I spent on dinner the day before--the one over which I had not stopped punishing myself. It turned out that God was a God of precision that day. Oh how blessed I was!

JIM'S PHONE CALL

February 2013 is a month that the State of Maine will never forget. Back to back blizzards and an additional snowstorm blasted the state on three consecutive Sundays. The first one dumped 30 inches of snow; the second between six and 10 inches and the third---I lost count. Oh my gosh! Everyone thought it would never stop snowing! There was a record- breaking accumulation of snow all totaled. The snow was piled three quarters of the way up on my vertical windows and that was not from any drifting. Gazing out my front window I was blinded by sparkling white snow everywhere I looked. The apartments were barely visible. The whole area appeared to be a snow covered meadow. It was like something I had never seen before.

The first thing in the morning following one of the storms, I moved my car to make room for the snow vehicles to plow. An available parking space near the closest curb was not to be found so I drove farther up and parked the car in the office parking lot and walked all the way back home. Plowing took place soon afterward. At 11 a.m. the Spirit of God impressed upon me to eat lunch. I impressed upon Him that I was not accustomed to eating my lunch at 11 o'clock in the morning. But-- I obeyed. I heated some leftover, homemade, deer chili in the microwave. Umm---good. After eating, I walked up to the office parking lot to retrieve my car and drove it back to my parking spot in front of my apartment. As soon as I parked and turned off the engine, my cell phone rang.

The caller was my friend, Jim, who had just returned from a missionary trip to South America. I knew that when he called we would be on the phone for a while as he related one story after another about his trip, and I would soak up every story as if I had been there with him. Having lived in a foreign country and having spent much time with Latino friends and acquaintances, I would visualize the terrain, the villages and the people. My traveling friend was breathing life into me. His timing was perfect--- or should I say God's timing was perfect? Had he called five minutes before or five minutes later it would not have been a good time. If I had not eaten my lunch an hour early as God led me to, I would not have been relaxed enough to enter into the amazing conversation we had. He knows the end from the beginning.

ALL THE TIME

On the way to church one morning an old friend of mine, Pat, who I had not seen or spoken to in at least four years was on my mind. I prayed for her and became occupied with thoughts of the last time we saw each other. Later at church my pastor's wife brought up a subject that reminded me of when my granddaughter was just a little girl and in Pat's Sunday school class. I even mentioned it to her. I made a mental note to try to connect with her when I returned home later that day.

Several hours later I returned home and went to my computer to retrieve my messages. Who did I receive a message from, but Pat, the very same friend who had been on my mind all morning long.

This type of happening takes place every, single week. As profound as God is, He still performs in very simple ways.

TWO HOURS EARLY

One Saturday afternoon at 4 o'clock I was working on my book while waiting to go to the clubhouse to open the doors for the concert at 6:00 p.m. that night. The Spirit of God spoke to me loudly telling me to go over to the clubhouse right then. It was only 4:15. I never went over at 4:15 but I knew He had to be telling me for a reason so I got all my stuff together--stereo and speakers, vases with flowers for decorations etc.-- and left to go across the street to the clubhouse. I walked to the driver's door of my car when I noticed a car pulling up. I looked around getting ready to wave to the driver as it was customary for the residents to wave even if we did not recognize the drivers. To my complete surprise, the woman in the passenger seat looked familiar. I glanced at her a second time and saw her glancing back at me as if she knew me. I got out of my car and walked over to the other car. What a surprise to see people I knew, Carol and John from my friend Pastor Tom's church from up the coast. They had come to the area to attend a memorial service and heard about the concert, and thought they would come to it before heading back up the coast. They realized they had come early, but their event was over with and they thought they would come to my event early as they had no idea where the community building was located. If they had not seen me they would have headed home.

If the Holy Spirit had not told me to leave my house much earlier than I ever had, there is no way that our spotting each other would have taken place. They would have headed home missing the concert. I can't say it enough: it is always God's impeccable, precise, perfect TIMING!

GOOD BYE WILLIE

On a Sunday afternoon in April of 2013 I received a phone call from my girlfriend, Joan, whom I had not seen since winter. We had talked on the phone and kept in touch via e-mail, but our schedules would not permit us to visit. When I conveyed to my friend that I had spent the biggest part of the winter in my room writing as walking had gotten to be a bigger problem for me, she felt bad and on the spur of the moment changed her plans and headed over to my apartment on her bicycle. It was wonderful to see her.

After we caught up with family news and such, Joan told me that she was going to buy a miniature bicycle/ car. She had me write down a website address to which I replied, "Let's check it out now". We went into my bedroom and to the computer where my eye caught a series of e-mail messages one of which was from my sister who had the day before returned from a cruise, and to whom I still had not spoken since her return. Before I had a chance to access Google, my eyes caught the first few words of the e-mail after my sister's name the words, 'I noticed in the obituaries…'oh dear…I wondered what news would follow.

I presumed she was referring to one of our late parents' elderly friends, and I said to Joan, "Let me see who it was that died, and then we will go to the Internet site so you could show me the bicycle/car". The next thing I knew I was reading the name of the deceased, and he wasn't one of my parents' friends at all. He was Willie K--- , the boy who lived next door to us when we grew up who was like a brother to us. He and my brother were best friends. The tears flowed (they still flow). He had been on my heart all through the years. Of course, all us kids in the neighborhood all drifted apart as the years went on, but he and his wife came to our parents' 50th anniversary party and to all the wakes in our family. I was extremely upset, and don't know how I would have fared had Joan not been there to comfort me.

Can you see the connection between the phone call from Joan and the spontaneous bike trip to my apartment on the same day that I received the news about someone for whom I deeply cared? What a compassionate God.

THE ACCIDENT

My youngest son was visiting me one summer when we took a ride to the wharf at the harbor in Portland, Maine. I was sitting in my car reading a book while my son went into a fishing supply store to purchase some supplies. I was totally relaxed focusing my attention between my book and the two seals partaking of a free banquet of fish from fishermen in nearby boats all in view of my car window.

The next thing I knew a big, rental truck came around the back side of the building failing to negotiate the turn, and plowed into the right rear fender of my car. Crunchhhhhh….oh what a horrible sound! The driver, with a look of uncertainty on his face, began to back up. I started hollering and beeping the horn in order for him to stop as I surmised that he would incur additional damage; I hoped my son would hear the horn and come running out. He did. I called the police who came out and wrote up a report. I was glad I was not hurt.

The following day my son and I went to two different auto body shops to have the damage estimated. Dealing with faxes and phone calls to and from the insurance company was an annoying inconvenience. Simultaneously, the brake pads went on my car. I had no money to pay for the parts. There was no way I was going to burden my family with this car problem after all they had already done for me.

Interestingly, two weeks before the accident with my car, I was praying for money (which I never do) and interestingly, when my car was hit, the immediate thoughts that came to my mind were that the only times I have ever been involved in an accident were when God wanted to bring something good to me from the accident. I wondered what it might be. I was soon to find out.

The person from the insurance company handling the claim called very early one morning. In fact, I was in the bathroom and still a little groggy when the phone rang. She said that she bargained with the auto body owner and they knocked off $100.00 from his estimate, and that they would be sending me a check, and that I could do whatever I wanted with it. What! What a shock! Well firstly, I surmised that there was strategy behind her calling me so early in the morning. I think she wanted to catch me when I was vulnerable. Secondly, I thought that her sending me the check rather than sending it to the auto body owner directly made me think that she was coercing me into giving her immediate consent to wrap up the deal over the phone, even though the estimate was a lower amount of money figuring that the (imaginary) dollar signs would be extremely tempting, and they were. Yet, as tempting as the money was-I could have used it to publish my book-what was more important was the common sense advice given to me by my sons, which was to have the damage fixed because when winter came the water and snow could ruin the inside/underside of my car and then I would be in big trouble. Ultimately, God led me to follow their advice.

I had a fellow from church order the brake pads and rotor for my car from the Internet. When they were delivered he replaced them for me. I paid him for his help which I'm sure saved me a couple of hundred dollars. With that job accomplished I had the rear fender replaced and all the damage on the car repaired. The bottom line is that had I not had that accident I would not have had the money to fix the brakes on my car. (Of course, my sons would have stepped up to the plate, yet I did not want them to know about my dilemma.) Again, God had all the bases covered.

CHAPTER 3

ANSWERED PRAYER

THE POWER OF PRAYER

I really cannot complain about allergic symptoms because I have had so few allergy attacks in quite a few years, but even infrequent bouts with the culprits have made me miserable. After being plagued with an annoying dry cough for several weeks during an awful bout with the beastly allergies one fall, and having the symptoms get so bad that I could not talk without coughing- an irritating nuisance- my prayer partner laid hands on me one day while we prayed at the river. Mary was a prayer warrior and when she prayed she prayed believing.

Throughout the course of the day the amount of my coughing actually lessened, and by evening I had not coughed at all; neither did I cough the following morning. I did what the woman with the issue of blood did in the New Testament, and grabbed hold of the hem of Jesus' garment and would not let go for dear life---desperation?---no---expectation!

God knew that I wanted to attend my ministry's regional conference in Massachusetts because I had not been able to attend in quite a span of time. Had I not been healed right away, my chances of going would have been nil. God brought about my healing. I was so thankful for His coming through for me. There is so much power in prayer and even more power when the Body lays hands on us. When praying for healings I always remember what I was taught which is that we pray firstly to bring glory to the Son of God, and secondly for our discomfort to be alleviated for our own sake.

BABY LIAM

My great-grandson Liam was born on December 23, 2011 in Connecticut. He had a few problems at first but he seemed to be doing o.k. after a couple of days so he was sent home, but not for long. The little guy started to experience severe medical problems and was taken to the Hartford Children's Hospital. From there he was transported by ambulance to a Boston children's hospital where he underwent heart surgery. Words to describe the emotions in our family during Liam's ordeal have not been discovered thus far. I don't think I have ever cried so hard in my life. I could not conceive of what his parents and grandparents were going through.

I did not know if my heartbreak meant that I was not resting in God's healing power; all I knew was that I associated with the poor, weak baby and felt his parents' pain.

E-mails and phone calls were transmitted, non-stop, several times a day from the hospital to family members. Strength as a family unit truly manifested itself in a notable way as we all connected with one another during all hours of the day and night. The power of love consolidated us. Baby Liam made substantial progress with each day. The doctors were amazing, unbelievably knowledgeable and highly skillful. Ultimately, it was God who saved my great-grandson, yet his team of doctors was highly instrumental in restoring him to health.

SAM'S FINANCES

In early 2013 I prayed with my friend Sam and had my church Body pray for God to do a miracle with his finances. I reminded him that God is full of surprises. He wasn't buying it; he was so depressed. A few days after I had everyone pray for Sam, I called him to see how things were going. He reported to me that his niece had called his deceased brother's wife, who inherited his brother's money, and told her that if her father, Sam's brother, were alive that he would have helped Sam. His sister-in-law agreed to give my friend a sizeable lump sum of money which would help him with a security deposit for an apartment and other pressing expenses and to get on his feet.

How many times do radical things like that happen? Nothing is too big for God.

AND YET ANOTHER BLESSING

Two months later I talked with Sam on the phone again, and we prayed together that God would open up a part time job for him. Two weeks after that we spoke on the phone again, and Sam was all excited to report that some new friends, businessmen, not only bought him a new pair of boots and groceries, but hired him to clean their shop for 10 hours a week.

Interestingly, business picked up for them and they were able to considerably increase Sam's working hours. A couple of months after that Sam sent me a picture e-mail of himself and his new family having a family time together in their home. It was exactly what Sam needed-not just a job, but to be a part of a family.

God went beyond/ beyond.

AN INSTANT REPRIEVE

To my adopted daughter: Did you pray for me a little while ago? I think you must have, but if not, I am sure I was on your heart because God has touched me. I have had no pain in over 10 minutes. It feels so wonderful...a blessed reprieve. SUCH RELIEF!!! And the best part is that you, the Body of Christ, my daughter, had everything to do with it!

Thank you for your heart. I love you---another testimony for my next book, and of course, for 'Tapping Into His Treasures' T.V. show. I love being a King's kid. Love you ...

XXOO, Mother

ELLIE'S JOB

On one of my friend Ellie's visits we discussed her losing her job. She had applied for a variety of positions with different companies, yet securing employment seemed hopeless--too few jobs, too many applicants. Her husband ran a business out of their house, but contemplated the belief that family and business did not mix, so she did not dare approach the subject of working for him. She and I brought it up to God when we prayed before she left to go home, however. We prayed precisely that her husband would at least give her a chance to work in his office. The following day Ellie e-mailed me to tell me that she acquired a job. God had come through and her husband hired her as his secretary.

DIVINE DEFINITION

For someone who rests in God as a way of life, I was bewitched into dwelling on a situation in a neighborhood I lived in during the 90's. A young neighbor continually called me for rides here and rides there. I was always sentimental and imagined how it would be for me if I didn't have a car; I ended up taking her on many errands. I never checked it with God except to complain to Him about the interruptions from my housework and writing schedule. How was I supposed to get done what He called me to do in the field of writing with the constant interruptions from my neighbors? The dilemma I was in was making me crazy. I felt guilty for feeling the way I did; I needed some clarification, some answers; I needed God's mind.

Two of my close friends prayed with me that God would give me definition for the situation. The Spirit of God was faithful in giving me some thoughts, but the dynamic answer He gave me was through a devotional I read at the exact time I was going through the problem. It read: Just like all things in life, giving has its limitations. Being too generous can have its toll. Your kindness might be taken advantage of, and people might abuse your good intentions. Beware of individuals who are continuously seeking your aid. It's better to teach them how to solve their problems than to always attend to their needs.

That was my definition. What a Faithful Friend!

MY FRIEND DELORES

My friend Delores from Massachusetts was in Maine visiting her sister Jayne in northern Maine in January of 2013 when she gave me a call asking if she could stop to visit me on her way back through the southern part of the state the following afternoon, Sunday. I wanted so much to see her because it had been a couple of years since we had last seen each other, and her husband had passed away just two months beforehand. "I have to go to Pastor Colby's surprise birthday party in Rockland tomorrow afternoon but I do want you to come. How about if I only stay at the party for an hour, and you leave your sister's a little later than you had planned, and we'll both meet at my apartment before it gets dark. We'll have the whole evening together to catch up and you could stay overnight." " I'll take you out for supper," said Delores.

I arrived home from the party at approximately 4 o'clock the next day and waited as patiently as I could for my friend to arrive. Dusk advanced so I called her cell phone even though I was nervous about her answering it while she was driving. I waited and I prayed. Then I remembered that all of my calls didn't always come through on my cell phone so I checked my voicemail. Sure enough she had left a message. I immediately called her back. She had pulled off the highway at the exit before mine, and pulled into a gas station/convenience store parking lot. She didn't have a clue where she was so I asked her to put the attendant on her phone so that I could talk with him for a minute. I asked him to please direct my friend to Maine Street, Brunswick instead of having her get back on the highway, and to tell her that I would meet her on Maine Street in front of Frosty's Donut Shop.

I left in a hurry for downtown. Within ten minutes a car with a Massachusetts plate pulled up beside me on Maine Street. I swiftly ran to my friend's car in the freezing cold. "Let's go to a restaurant right now before we go to your house", Delores said. "O.K., the restaurant is right down the street. Follow me." I was so relieved that she had arrived in Brunswick without any hitches.

We bore a striking resemblance to two icicles as we hurried from our cars to the back entrance to the restaurant. As soon as our boots touched the plush carpeting we rode the elevator to the main floor. As we exited the elevator we entered the bar section of the restaurant where a few sets of eyes gazed at a big T.V. screen watching a playoff football game. Delores was the first to spot a big, rustic fireplace with an inviting fire that called our names. "Can we sit there?" she hollered to the hostess. "Sure". An attractive, mahogany table surrounded by large, black, leather comfortable- looking chairs was situated right in front of the fireplace. The warmth helped us to thaw out; it felt so good. At last we were together face to face and I could minister God's love to my friend in person rather than over the phone.

Before we even glanced at the menus that the waitress placed before us, I reached over and held Delores' hand saying softly, "How are you doing since David passed?" "I'm doing well. I am so confident that he is in heaven that I have had no reason to shed tears or to grieve these past two months". Then, within seconds after she spoke those words, I don't know if it was because of the beauty of the flames from the fireplace; from the softness of my hand grasping her hand; from the presence of God that surrounded us, or if it was a combination of all three, but suddenly a deluge of tears gushed out of my friend's eyes. The emotion came from deep down in her soul and she cried and cried. She dabbed her eyes with a tissue which quickly became saturated whereby the kind waitress brought over a box of tissues caringly placing them on the seat next to Delores and slipping away.

I realized in my heart of hearts that my friend was strong and was walking closely with God, yet I also realized that we all have tender hearts, and I suspected that there must have been tears bottled up somewhere inside her. I had prayed that sooner or later God would release those tears--and He did.

A divine healing had taken place right before my eyes. I was not the one grieving, yet it was revealed to me through the powerful scene what Godly friendships are all about.

WORKING FROM HOME

As most everyone I know can identify with, feelings of despair due to insufficient finances have shown their ugly heads on hundreds of occasions throughout my lifetime. Living on a fixed income with barely anything left over at the end of the month can cause a person to feel somewhat helpless and hopeless at times. Expenses for persons on social security are the same every month; however, each month brings additional expenses of its own. Money that we tuck away for yearly expenses like car registrations and computer protection programs which come due bi-annually often is borrowed to purchase birthday and Christmas gifts; an occasional hostess gift; a luncheon or any number of things. Try as we may to plan for the expected and the unexpected, our attempts are futile; it cannot be done. I am appreciative that there is enough money to pay my bills; yet, sometimes I get a little 'down' because there is seldom enough money to go fun shopping, on outings or on trips.

On one of those occurrences I was feeling gloomy because of such a financial state of being, when I started to pray about getting a part time job although I had no peace about it for the following reasons: I had been devoting my whole existence, all my time, energy and a sizeable amount of money to the work of the Lord for a big part of my life. The thoughts of having to dip into this sacred time was extremely troublesome to me; the constant, severe pain I am always in will not allow me to walk, stand or sit still for more than 15 minutes at a time unless I place an ice pack on my lower back (more recently a tens unit); subsidized housing would automatically take one third of my pay check, and with taxes I would virtually be working and experiencing more pain for naught. Yet, I could not see even a glimpse of an escape from my dilemma. I kept asking God to drop money out of the sky so that I would not have to work, but the only thing falling out of the sky was snow, rain and hail.

The following day I went to church expecting an answer from God as to whether I should or should not follow through with my plan to work. Pastor Ron, the assistant pastor, gave the introduction. He asked where our focus was and quoted from the Book of Luke. He also stated that 'God would provide', and he prompted us to obey God in 'everything'. Pastor Wally admonished us to be cautious in making big decisions. He also reiterated some of the things that Pastor Ron shared.

The first thing of which I was cognizant was that two stories relayed to me by people who tried to interest me in working from home were just curve balls. I made up my mind right then to obey God and to change my mind about getting a job. I would trust Him implicitly to provide for me and for His work.

A few hours later my friend Elaine stopped by my apartment on her way back home to Massachusetts from her house in Maine. Her visit was wonderful, as always. Her other half went out to the van in an attempt to get Elaine moving because he wanted to hit the road. She and I had a special two minutes in my dinette whereupon she pulled out her wallet and began to fish through some paper. She yielded what appeared to be a $20.00 bill and placed it on the table at which point I tried to give it back to her. In tears she told me that God had told her a month prior to mail me the money but she had forgotten. "This is not from me", she said, "it is from God". I thanked her from the bottom of my heart. I cut a hunk of homemade coffee cake and wrapped it for my guests to take with them, and while Elaine was in the rest room, I went outside to pet her dog while I waited for her. Hugs and kisses were prolific alongside the van with a prayer for safe traveling. When I went back into the house, the money that Elaine tucked underneath the centerpiece on the table came into view. I picked it up looking more closely at it and discovered that it was a $100.00 bill; I was in shock! What a blessing! The pressure I had been under instantly dissolved.

I was precisely where I was supposed to be that morning. God spoke to me through His anointed pastors. This is a prime example of following the pastor/teacher to whom God has called us. I made a calculated decision to forfeit going to work, and to trust God to provide for my wants and needs as well as for His ministries.

I had been fasting that day unbeknownst to anyone. It never fails that every time I fast something monumental takes place in my life. God brought glory to His Son, He honored me and He blessed my friend for her generosity…no question about it.

ALL-NIGHT PRAYER

The All-Night Prayer Chain on Facebook, launched by my friend Christina, is a site where many Christians from around the world go to share prayer requests and to offer up prayers for others. The number of times that God has answered these prayers is beyond counting. Included in these prayers was a corporate prayer that He would hold off the executions of two pastors who were imprisoned and tortured in overseas prisons. God has come through a number of times. In addition to one pastor's life being spared, he was eventually released from prison. Regarding the second pastor, his execution date has been postponed.

Many of the participants in all-night prayer sacrifice many hours of sleep in order to pray corporately with fellow Christians. The magnitude of power released from heaven when many come together one in Spirit is insurmountable. This should make everyone desire to be a part of a vision.

A MOM AND DAUGHTER MAKE UP

A friend of mine who I connected with after over 30 years came to visit me one day during which time she opened up to me about being estranged from her daughter for many years. She wept as she expressed her love for the young woman; her heartache was weighty from the pressing situation. God came over us and we found ourselves amidst a Holy Spirit visitation in my living room that day. I began to pray at once laying hands on my friend in proxy for her daughter. I prayed for a spirit of reconciliation to come to them both. The release of heaviness to my friend was instantaneous. We rested in the finished work of the Lord pertaining to the prayer I prayed.

Within a few weeks I received the call that I expected; the reconciliation had taken place. To God be the glory.

A QUICK ANSWER

While listening to my assistant pastor preach at church one Sunday morning, I was almost completely certain that the Holy Spirit was speaking directly to me about my ministries. I said to Him, "Lord, I believe that You are speaking to me, not just generally, but specifically, and if You are, would You confirm that You are by having the pastor mention Hudson Taylor's name in his message? (Hudson Taylor was a famous missionary to China a long time ago). I wrote down my request in my steno pad as I silently spoke it to Him. Within three minutes the pastor mentioned Hudson Taylor's name in his message. He could have mentioned one of thousands of missionaries, yet he chose to mention Hudson Taylor's name!

Do God's confirmations get any more direct than that????

Is prayer answered any more quickly than that????

Praise Him!!!!

HONOR

One time when I had to make a major decision about something, I prayed for God to give me divine definition. One Sunday afternoon in between morning church and evening church, I turned on a Christian T.V. channel. I immediately started to change the channel because I wasn't crazy about the message that a certain preacher was preaching. And then it was as if God grabbed the remote from out of my hand-- 'Leave it on', I heard the Holy Spirit say; so I did.

The T.V. pastor spoke on honor---honoring our parents, our pastors and anyone else that we needed to honor. My question to God was, "Am I dishonoring someone, Lord, that You want me to hear this message?" God replied to me in my spirit saying, 'It is not that you are dishonoring anyone, it is that you are not giving the proper honor to someone that you ought to be honoring.' I searched my heart and there it was in front of me. Aside from God bringing it to my attention, I would not have picked up on the sin of omission because I had been blinded to it. "Help me, Lord. Help me to give these people honor on purpose".

The following morning the Lord did something amazing. He spoke to me with clear definition regarding plans for my future. I had been praying for a few months for clear definition pertaining to something. Do you get the connection? He waited until my heart was pure before He blessed me by answering my specific prayer…but bless me, He did.

SNUGGLING WITH DAD

A friend who had been racked with pain for months e-mailed me one evening to tell me that she could not bear the pain any longer. I ministered God's compassion to her through an e-mail, and prayed for her intermittently that evening. The extent of my own pain was debilitating as well that day, and so I took a break from sitting at the computer which always exacerbates my pain and I watched a movie. In the first scene of the movie a young girl was sleeping in her bed when a terrible thunder and lightning storm awakened her; she was terrified. She grabbed her teddy bear, ran out of her room and into her parents' room begging them to let her get into bed with them. Her father, expressing heartfelt understanding, pulled down the covers motioning for his daughter to get under the covers between him and her mother.

I put the movie on pause and e-mailed the woman these words: 'All I could think of as I watch this movie is you, my friend, with this storm going on in your life. All I could visualize is our heavenly Daddy pulling down the covers for you to crawl in bed next to Him.

The e-mail I received back from my friend conveyed warm appreciation for taking the time to share God's heart with her. The words of the e-mail became life to her gravitating all the way to her soul and bringing her divine comfort and compassion. Her response revealed to me how quickly the Lord was able to touch a soul--her soul.

Stories like the above take place several times every week of the year. Yes, God is in the business of answering prayers, touching souls and restoring lives.

MY BFF

Sometimes we have to wait a long time for God to answer our prayers, but answer He does. For decades I had been praying for my lifelong friend to get an interest in learning more about the Bible. We have had hundreds of spiritual conversations over the phone, but that was it. Decades later the call came, "I have something to tell you", she said. "I am going to a Bible study. I am learning all about the Apostle Paul". You can imagine my sheer delight!

MY FRIEND'S SON

My friend's son was stopped by the police for erratic driving and charged with O.U.I. (operating under intoxication). Because my friend is a child of God and prays non-stop for her son, whether he was right or wrong did not make a difference as to whether God would show up in the situation.

My friend e-mailed me to tell me that her son's boss thought he was a good kid and wanted to do all he could to help. The employer actually went with her to meet a lawyer the following morning. He also posted bail of either $500.00 or $1,000.00. He said he would have her son work it off. He told my friend that he had always wanted a younger brother and was glad to help.

Help like this isn't just floating around this planet. Concerned people are not waiting to dispense money to people they barely know. The man had to be influenced by God.

BEFRIENDED

For a period of three weeks I prayed about trying to get in touch with a former friend from across the country that I had not seen or talked with in over 25 years. I had been challenged to become involved in a situation concerning her, and I thought it was God Who challenged me.

I did not want to do something outside of God's will so I simply asked Him for divine definition and guidance. During this time of prayer, my old friend contacted me on Facebook requesting friendship. A door opened and I walked in. It is so easy with God.

THE PAIN MESSAGE

You would think that after suffering from pain for over 35 years that a person would get used to it and not come undone over it. Well, I have adapted to the constant pain that besets me, yet as things go, I became victim to an isolated event of succumbing to the pain one winter day in March of 2013 when my mind and emotions disguised the strong person I had been up until that point.

I made an appointment with an orthopedic doctor who ordered physical therapy and x-rays. The x-rays revealed that my Scoliosis had worsened and that my spine was at a 45 degree angle in the shape of the letter V pushing outward from my back. No wonder I was in agony. And that was just one of several back conditions plaguing me including Spondylitis which was the cause of the cartilage in my lumbar area disintegrating. Severe arthritis and osteoporosis played their parts; I had trouble sitting; I had trouble standing; I could hardly use the keyboard anymore. One day it got to me and I couldn't even pray. I did not feel God's presence. I did not know if I could bear the pain for another minute. Cloudiness replaced sound thinking in my head.

That night I watched my Baltimore church service on the Internet. After a week long absence, my head pastor got up to preach. He had spent most of the preceding week in a horizontal position due to horrific nosebleeds for which his nose had to be packed. Because of his condition his mind was wrapped around pain. Pain was the theme of his message to the church. He encouraged us that one day there would be no more pain. His message touched me like no other message could possibly have touched me. I felt God's grace pouring into my soul. I was able to rise above my circumstances. God was so precise. I once again felt God's presence. I was myself again.

THE INJECTION

March of 2113 was the first time I had ever asked for prayer before I went in for a spinal injection and WOW! What a difference it made! Nearly 50 Facebook friends commented on my page that they would pray that it wouldn't be bad for me. The night before my scheduled doctor visit coincided with the Facebook all -night monthly prayer meeting so I had even more friends praying for me. I was completely covered with prayer by the time I went to the doctor's the next day.

Even though I knew God would be there for me, the shot I received a few years earlier was so horrific that I wondered to what degree it would be decreased because of the prayers. It turned out that I never felt any of the three separate shots I received. God was there with me.

EVERY HOUR ON THE HOUR

In the winter of 2013 my prayer life drastically changed. A very special friend of mine who I think of as my daughter was going through intense pain due to a medical condition she had for a prolonged period of time. I remembered that in my past I would pray every hour on the hour for emergencies and for pressing issues, even setting my alarm clock for every hour on the hour. I remembered some of the ways that God answered those every hour on the hour prayers sometimes within hours. I decided to pray for my daughter/friend in that same way. Then another very important prayer request came in and I added that person to my list. Then I added my kids to my list even though I pray for them each morning. Then another family member was having a family problem so I added that person to my list. Then my next door neighbor was having a problem with her son so I added him to my hourly list. Then I had company from northern Maine who was getting to the end of herself so I added her to my list. Then my cousin's daughter came down with cancer and I added her to my list. Then a distant relative came down with cancer and I added her to my list. Then I was contacted by the mother of one of my little charges from back in the early 2,000's regarding her son and I counted it a privilege to put him on my hourly list.

My list has grown and I have prayed for all these people so many times that I have memorized the order in which I pray for them. I only set the alarm clock during night hours on occasions of pressing importance, but I have tried to set it during waking hours every hour on the half hour unless I am out doing errands or attending church. I am not as faithful to set the clock as I was the first year; nevertheless, I continue to pray intermittently throughout every day for these dear ones.

update: My church members and I have been praying for the daughter of one of our own who has had a death threat on her life *from an extremely rare disease. She needed a tremendous amount of funds for necessary surgery. The situation was impossible, yet the Bible says that nothing is impossible for God, and so it was that our endless prayers were answered when the young woman received an anonymous gift for $50,000.00 toward the surgery.*

My friends and I prayed believing for a miracle for my friend's daughter who had kidney problems and was told by doctors that she could not go through a pregnancy. The young woman dreamed of becoming a mother for most of her life. Three years after her marriage her kidney problems diminished and she gave birth to a healthy baby boy.

GETTING BACK MY E-MAIL ADDRESS

When I moved from Warren, Maine to Brunswick, Maine I had to change my Internet service provider because my company did not service the Brunswick area. That meant that I had to give up my e-mail address which I absolutely loved. It was like pulling teeth for me to give it up. I prayed that I would one day be able to get it back again even though I did not have the faith that it would ever happen.

Eighteen months later when I moved from Brunswick south to another town near the New Hampshire border, my Brunswick Internet service provider did not service the area I moved to so I had to go back to my original service provider. After the technician set up the cable he started to fill out some paper work, and asked me to pick an e-mail address for my account. I casually told him that I had to give up the one I loved, and really had not thought about getting another since I obtained an e address for my Google g mail account. He wanted me to pick a new address for the new company. Just for the heck of it he punched in my old address to see if it was still available. I could not imagine it still being available since it was one that many writers sought after; yet, lo and behold---it was available. God gave it back to me. I was stunned!

CHAPTER 4

CONFIRMATION

PURPOSE

Five hours after videoing a show on the theme of, 'purpose', I sat down to work on my manuscript. I resumed at Chapter Seven exactly at this portion:

Insight: #1and #2… Solomon entered into counsel with his mind… Ecclesiastis 1:16. In Ecclesiastis 2:1 it reads: "I said in my mind"… these two verses depict that God's Spirit meets our spirit in our minds, and that we should 'on purpose' enter into counsel with Him in our minds.

The next morning for my devotional God gave me Proverbs 4:25, "Let your eyes look right on with fixed purpose, and let your gaze be straight before you. The portions in Ecclesiastes and the words 'fixed purpose' were confirmations that the theme I spoke on that week was in alignment with God's mind.

It is a part of God's character to give us confirmation concerning what He leads us to do. Ask yourselves: Wouldn't you like God to confirm something that you say or do? You know that you know, yet to hear Him back you up takes any guessing out of the equation.

MY FRIEND'S FRIEND

Friends and acquaintances often bring friends to my house to meet me. During one of these times one of the visitors was getting ready to make some unwise choices in her life beginning that very night. She was also caught up in a maze of crazy episodes occurring in her family. I certainly had a lot going through my mind, and I certainly didn't know her well enough to express my opinions; yet, I was listening very carefully to the Holy Spirit and knew that He was the One putting the thoughts in my mind. I was under an unction to allow Him to use me as His mouthpiece. I, therefore, opened my mouth and voiced what the Lord wanted me to say cautioning the woman and giving her advice.

 After the women left I was still wishy-washy about my boldness in counseling one of the women visiting me and in giving her unsolicited advice. I opened my Bible and this is what God gave me: Jeremiah 17:16 b, "Thou knowest all that hast passed my lips…it was approved by Thee."….I was blown away!

PRECISION

One morning at a tenant's meeting at the complex in which I used to reside, a woman named Verna sat at the same table as me. I knew that she had been a chaplain at a prison in Maine earlier in her life, and since I have a background in prison ministry, I initiated a conversation with her. I mentioned that I once had a friend named Barbara whom I used to visit in prison. That same night God led me to a portion in my Bible which happened to be underlined. It spoke of visiting someone in prison. Written in the border was the name Barbara with a date (you really have to visualize this). This was one and the same as the woman named Barbara whom I had spoken of to Verna that morning. God was telling me that He was right there in our presence and in our conversation earlier in the day....praise GOD!

OLD TESTAMENT PROPHETS

One day I produced a T.V. show that had to do with Old Testament prophets. I was intrigued to learn about the prophecies of which they spoke pertaining to Jerusalem and the temple. That same night I watched a documentary about Jerusalem being the covenant city; it was like the cream on the pudding. The following day I told my friends that I would have to do a sequel to the prophet show. They agreed.

The following night before going to bed, I watched Christian T.V. which I only watch occasionally before retiring for the night. What did the T.V host talk about but Jerusalem and the predictions that the Prophet Haggai made about the temple.....unbelievable! I couldn't have orchestrated that if I tried; it was all Him.

GO HIGHER WITH GOD

 One day the Lord reminded me that it is His will for us to go higher with Him in His plan. His voice was so loud that I did a show that very day on that same theme. What a privilege to pass on to others what God has passed on to me. Going to the highest level in Christendom not only draws us closer to the Lord, it blesses Him. He also reminded me not to settle, but to take on more T.V. stations for my Christian show. That same night my pastor spoke on the same topic--going higher with God. That is what I call a confirmation!

He also made the following statement: David did not know that 1,000 years after he lived, someone would address the Messiah as 'the Son of David'. It is the same with those of us today who are called. We need to take callings seriously.

I'M A MISFIT

After spending some time with people who made a number of insinuations about my beliefs and my church, I said to God, "Lord, I feel like such a misfit when I am with these people". A minute later I turned on Christian T.V. to clear my mind. As happens from time to time someone was preaching who I could not handle, and without even listening to his subject I was quick to pick up the remote to change the channel. 'Don't change the channel; leave it on,' is what I heard God say loudly and clearly.

These were the next words that came from the preacher's mouth (and he was a hollerin and pointing his finger): *'SO YOU THINK YOU'RE A MISFIT –DO YOU? WELL I'LL TELL YOU WHAT! JESUS CAME TO MAKE YOU A MISFIT! HE DIDN'T COME TO BRING PEACE. HE CAME TO BRING A SWORD---FAMILY MEMBER AGAINST FAMILY MEMBER'.*

Only God could cause something like that to happen. Divine orchestration was put into play for my benefit.

SARCASTIC JABS

I am not writing this testimony to make sport of something troublesome that used to bother me. I'm writing it because I know it will help others. I choose stories and testimonies that I think readers will associate with, and who God could help to draw closer to Himself.

While fresh insinuations that were flung at me were mulling through my mind, I reminded God how that year after year that the same type of mudslinging was taking place at a certain type of gathering. I could not put my finger on what to call the insinuations. I knew that I was not responsible for even the slightest rift, and that the damaging words were not a figment of my imagination. That same day I watched yet another preacher on T.V. who ended his message by referring to unkind slurs as 'sarcastic jabs'. I jumped off the couch and threw my hands up in the air thanking God for hitting the nail right on the head. There it was--the term that I couldn't put my finger on for half of my life---sarcastic jabs! I felt as if I had gone through a lengthy court trial threatened with a lifelong incarceration, and instead, a verdict of 'not guilty' was handed down to me.

He knows; He sees; He cares…

NO WEAPON

As nasty words and comments continued to come at me and as I was being wrongfully accused, God led me to this Bible verse: "No weapon formed against you shall prosper".

SHARING GOD'S HEART

As I pointed out in a previous story, I am not including the following happening in my book to make sport of it either, but to help readers in their individual growth.

God put it on someone's mind to call me for help with a pressing situation which involved a possible eviction. She needed professional advice; yet, had no money to hire anyone, plus she had very few friends or contacts. Helping the woman was important to me because I too had been without a place to live a few times in my life and those were extremely difficult times. I was prepared to use my grocery money if I had to in order to obtain legal advice. I was strongly cautioned by those close to me not to get involved. There they were again---those words--- you can't get involved. I had heard them spoken by my father all my life ever since I was young. No one seemed to understand. I identified with the caregiver. As a caregiver myself I had cleaned many adult behinds, seriously the most unpleasant job in the whole world. I identified with her concerns about her future. My being there to support her, in my estimation, was not getting in the middle of things; it was the right thing to do.

My emotions were frazzled but I made it through the day, and awoke the following morning getting on my knees for God's mind on the situation, and then going straight to my Bible for a word from Him. Proverbs 31:26 is what I was given: 'She opens her mouth in skillful and godly wisdom, and on her tongue is the law of kindness (giving counsel and instruction). Proverbs 31: 8, 'Open your mouth for those unable to speak for themselves for the rights of all who are left desolate and defenseless'. 'Proverbs 31: 9, 'Open your mouth and judge righteously and administer justice for the poor and needy'.

My thoughts were in sync with the living God. What a release for my heavy heart. What a boost for my heart and soul. God's compassion was displayed through me, a vessel. What a privilege. What an honor.

CONFIRMATION FROM ALLAN

I am a follower of my friend Allan's daily devotionals on Facebook and you tube. We are so close in our thinking that occasionally there are times when I will produce a show one day and the following morning he will write about the same theme on his blog. For example, when I produced a show on 'division in the church', the following morning the theme for his daily blog was 'division in the church'.

REMINISCE

One time I did a T.V. show on the theme, 'memories,' in which I mentioned a popular magazine called 'Reminisce'. Later that afternoon after videoing the show and burning it to D.V.D.'s, I went to get my mail. What do you suppose was in my mailbox? A letter from the Reminisce magazine office was in my mail receptacle. The funny part of it was that I had not subscribed to the magazine in years. They wanted to know if I wanted to renew my subscription. How could that notice possibly have arrived in my mailbox after a few years on the same day that I wrote about that same magazine unless God orchestrated the timing of it?

GOD'S VOICE

Once when my schedule was jam -packed and I started to feel pressured, I realized that I would have to consider my mental and physical health in taking on more counseling and favors. The next day (not a week later, but the next day) I read in the Gospel of Mark 3:9 where Jesus told the disciples to have a little boat ready so that the crowd would not press hard on Him and crush Him. I believe that God gave me that passage referring to my emotional health from extending myself way too much.

STRONGHOLDS

It was Easter week and I was producing my weekly show. The Holy Spirit did not give me a theme about the resurrection of Christ to teach on that day. He told me instead to teach on the theme of 'strongholds' of the devil. I obeyed. He gave me John 8:37-59 to read verbatim from His Word where He described certain people as being of their father, the devil.

That evening I watched my Baltimore church's Easter play via the Internet. In one of the scenes Jesus and the Pharisees were having the same dialogue that I spoke on that morning taken from the exact, same Scriptures, John 8. For me it was riveting, an absolute confirmation.

BARABBAS

After working on a T. V. show theme having to do with Barabbas for several days and printing it out one afternoon, that very night my pastor spoke on Barabbas as the theme for his Wednesday night message. He used the name Barabbas as a synonym for the world system.

This confirmation was from God even though I never asked for it. He is so faithful.

SECOND BY SECOND

I was troubled about something and mulling it around my mind for days, and I needed to deal with it as soon as possible. I decided to call my mentor to ask if she could give me some enlightenment on the concerns with which I was heavy laden, or if she would at least pray about my situation. She didn't seem to be getting anything from the Holy Spirit at first, and wasn't going to conjure up an answer just for the sake of satisfying me, so we both remained quiet for a moment. Then she said to me that God may be taking me into a new phase of life whereby He wasn't going to tell me things ahead of time, but would take me on a path that was moment by moment. I was satisfied with her answer. "I wonder if He will give me confirmation on that as He often gives me confirmation on things," I asked, "although it's perfectly o.k. if He doesn't".

A few days later, a Sunday, God kept reminding me to watch my ministry's Sunday night service on the Internet which would be a special treat since I am usually in church on Sunday evenings and don't get to see the Baltimore service live.

The time came to tune in and a man whom my head pastor asked to give the introduction was at the pulpit. He shared something very beautiful. While the audience applauded, the man took his seat. But then my pastor asked him to go back up and to give his testimony. The man humbly told his story about having been addicted to alcohol since he was a young teenager, and how his addiction got tremendously out of hand as he got older. He went on to give shocking details of how his life turned out.

Then he shared with the listeners about how he came to know the ministry and how he began to follow Christ. He said that even though he had a new found faith and many new friends in the church, it was still a monumental effort to follow God. He said he vacillated for a long time. When he finally went all the way with Christ which did not happen overnight, his eyes were wide open and he could see how that he couldn't even go day by day any longer, and not even moment by moment, but second by second.

Those are the words that God wanted to use to impress upon me....second by second. They were a confirmation of my mentor, Sylvia's, words 'moment by moment' only He took them a little farther....second by second. An amazing confirmation.

CHAPTER 5

OBEDIENCE

CHRISTIAN CONCERTS

Coordinating concerts is not always an easy task as there are always last minutes changes with the musicians and with the use of facilities. I could only dream about having the performers' names written on my yearly schedule months ahead of time instead of having them tell me that they can't plan a few months in advance, but I guess that would cancel out the faith that I have to exercise each time they present me with bad or uncertain news. I can't get over how many times God has come through for us.

On one of those occasions one of our two regular groups could not make it which meant that even though I had a singer lined up, that we had no equipment on which to play his accompaniment C.D.'s. I had to search for someone with sound equipment. A past performer who did not have sound equipment, but had a guitar and sang for us came to mind. I called him and he happily agreed to perform. I did a happy dance as I wrote his name on my schedule as a definite. The following day I did an unhappy dance as I had to erase his name when he called me to tell me that his wife had made plans for that weekend unbeknownst to him.

I decided to leave it in the Lord's hands and not to worry about it. I knew He had something wonderful planned for the concert. The following week I called my neighbor to ask if she would be interested in playing her keyboard for a community sing-a-long. Although she loved to play, she wasn't comfortable enough to play in front of people. "What about my son, Jim?" she asked (I was hoping she would bring him up). We had been stuck without music once before when she called her son to bring his guitar and to help us out. At that time he accompanied a number of singers. I called Jim and placed his name on my concert schedule. I kept expressing praise and thanks to God knowing that something good was going to happen. And it did.

The night of the concert arrived, a cold, snowy night. We were blessed to have a small crowd show up on such a night. Jim dutifully accompanied all the singers providing tremendous pleasure to the audience. After one such selection I nonchalantly asked Jim if he sang, and if so, if he had any numbers he would like to share with us. Well, it happened that he not only sang but also wrote songs, one of which was his personal testimony of how God transformed his life. Included in his repertoire was a really funny song. The audience went wild over it. God proved Himself, yet again. And, if the performance wasn't more than enough, Jim, after hearing of our dilemma concerning sound equipment, told me that he owned sound equipment, and that any time I needed to borrow it to just give him a call. Amazing!

ANOTHER CONCERT

I had lots of church friends heading to Brunswick from three different directions for the Saturday night concert. Everything seemed uncomplicated until the day before. I asked my pastor and his wife if they could come early so that I could interview him for my T.V. show before the concert. Then I found out that someone in my complex passed away that week, and the family was using the clubhouse for a reception after the funeral of the deceased. I could only pray that their group would be out of the room (no disrespect) before the concert people started to arrive. In addition, the performers called the night before telling me that they would have to arrive a half hour earlier than usual to set up and practice. I would have to exercise nothing less than the faith of Jesus to believe that my plans would be accomplished. God would come through; I knew He would. That is what makes for an exciting life.

SAM

In January of 2013 I drove to Manchester, New Hampshire to have lunch with a friend of mine. He had been released from prison a few months earlier after serving time for over 20 years. I was introduced to him by a chaplain friend of mine when I was a religious volunteer in a Maine prison in the early 90's. I sang at the chapel services at that time. Sam talked with the chaplain about me having a private visit with him. It was not something I normally did at the big house. I only made an exception when the chaplain was effective in getting a 50 something year-old inmate who had never agreed to a visit with anyone because of fear of people to agree to have a visit with me. Because that visit was so highly successful, changing the inmate's life and transforming him, I thought I would make another exception and visit with Sam. Initially, we were placed in small cubicles situated off the expansive visiting area, but a few years later we were permitted to visit amidst all the inmates and their family members and friends. It turned out that I was Sam's only visitor in the 20 some odd years he was incarcerated. We have stayed in touch all through the years. He has been like a fifth son to me.

After his release and placement into an apartment building, I bought Sam an inexpensive microwave oven with only 700 watts because he had no kitchen facilities in the room he rented, and could not even enjoy a hot cup of coffee. I also made him a care package by filling a laundry basket full of household and cleaning items I collected from going through my cupboards and kitchen drawers and bathroom cabinet. I had hesitations about driving to New Hampshire because of severe back pain with which I was beset, yet I brought a stash of ice packs with me and I was on my way.

Manchester, having many one way streets, made finding Sam's street murder. I drove around and around as we connected with one another via our cell phones. Finally, I saw someone walking toward me that turned out to be Sam. He noticed me; it wasn't the other way around. He had changed so much that I drove right by him before he flagged me down.

My wish was to take him to a nice restaurant and to order him a big steak, but his wish was to take me to his favorite diner which served only fast food; I complied. He settled for pizza and I settled for just a plain hot dog in order to save room for a piece of apple pie. Lunch hardly mattered though; we were enjoying each other's company on the 'outside'. We could hardly believe that the time had finally come that he had talked and dreamed about for so long --his release from captivity, his re-entering the world that he had known when he was a young man; it was surreal. Apprehension accompanied his excitement because of the changes which had taken place in society over the 20 years he was away. He wondered how he would make the tremendous adjustment especially with his medical problems; his concerns were justified.

Our two-hour lunch was carefree. Surprisingly, neither of us talked a blue streak as I thought we would. Our time together was quiet, yet intense. After lunch I drove Sam to his place and he made two trips to his third floor apartment with the items I brought him. We bid each other goodbye hoping that too long a time wouldn't pass before we could get together again. Finding my way to the highway was a nightmare. Although I had specific directions from the locals, I still ended up driving back and forth totally disoriented, and finally had to stop at a gas station to ask an attendant for directions.

After I returned home Sam called to see if I made it home o.k. He was reeling from all his little surprises in the laundry basket. The biggest surprise was the small, colorful rooster that I stuck in the basket on a whim. My sister had given it to me and told me to give it away if I didn't want it. Well, I'm a rooster person, but I have so many that I couldn't even squeeze it into my small kitchen. My friend communicated to me over the phone that the rooster figurine had put a smile on his face because when he was a kid he spent a lot of time at his grandparents' farm and they had roosters that were the same color as the one I gave him. One rooster he named Mike and the ceramic figure I gave him looked just like Mike. I was jumping for joy in my spirit that a man could get such happiness from a rooster figurine. I told him that I thought that he would think I was a fruitcake for putting the rooster in the basket with the rest of the stuff; there surely was a lesson in that.

The next thing he told me was that he had been meaning to pick up a cleaning cloth and kept forgetting to do so. I had found one in my drawer that was brand new and in a wrapper. Little did I know that something so insignificant could make Sam's day. He told me that he could not believe what he was seeing when he saw the tube of 'Close Up' toothpaste. He said that it was the only kind of toothpaste he liked and that only God could have known that. I told him that it was the only kind I have used for many years. He was also very excited about the Jesus of Nazareth D.V.D. and the Bible I enclosed. He had a private Christmas with God that day. What a blessing!

KAIROS

I was planning to have a 'down day' one Saturday until the phone rang around 9:30 a.m. The caller was an old friend who was in town to attend a Kairos meeting of prisoners, ex-prisoners, group leaders and volunteers. There went my unwinding day, yet I knew that God wanted me to give up my comfort to glorify Him, so I went to meet my friend and to join his group for a short period of time. It was great hooking up with my old friend. The larger group broke into groups of two which enabled my friend and I to reminisce about his family and our mutual friends, plus he brought photos for me to view. A new friend of mine, a pastor whom I had met when I moved to Brunswick, happened to be in the group, as well. I was pleasantly surprised when he stood up and told the group of my many years in prison ministry and about the concerts that I coordinate in the area. The blessings did not stop there. After the meeting I went to the shopping center and while shopping I found something for which I had been looking for a long time--a blessing from God for having given of myself. We give of our time, we put God first, and it always comes back to us.

MY UNCLE

My uncle lived clear across the country in California. I had prayed for him many times; yet, I had never known him to go to church or to even mention God so I did not know anything about his spiritual temperature. He was a wild man when he was in his prime, driving a pink Cadillac convertible and a motorcycle while sporting a black, leather jacket and black gloves. He had a different gal sitting beside him in his hot car every night, and when a favorite song came on the radio he would turn it up full blast and jump out of the car with his date and start dancing the swing dance when they were stopped at red lights. He taught me to drive when I was 13 years old. I was the envy of all my friends.

It was easy to say, 'God bless you, when I spoke with him on the phone, but I never had the nerve to witness to him. That is until God told me to call my uncle and to give him the plan of salvation. Believe me, there wasn't a half of one percent of myself in that phone call; it was all God. Anticipating up- front rejection, I was completely dumbfounded when my uncle not only responded to the gospel message, but hollered loudly and repeatedly, "Yes, yes, that is what I have always wanted". Had I known it would have been such a piece of cake, I would have presented the gospel to him decades beforehand. However, God's timing turned out to be precise and perfect--- my uncle met his Lord.

My uncle passed away several months after that. I am so thankful that I obeyed God.

INVEST

It kept coming and coming…the nudge to take on more stations, stations with many more viewers. The straw that broke the camel's back; the push that got me to take a step of action was my friend's post on Facebook. She shared a portion from a nationally known preacher, someone whom I loved and respected. I went to his website and listened to his message for that day. He spoke about the early days of his ministry and of how he wanted to keep it small (cough-cough). He spoke of feeling comfortable with a small ministry and safe from the attacks he would face had he expanded (cough-cough). He spoke of struggling with God for a long time (cough- cough). His whole message was geared to me. I could not resist God any longer.

The next day I sent a number of cover letter e-mails to several T.V. stations. I only received a few responses (this is typical). Having had my shows aired on several stations for 3 1/2 years cost a large amount of money for postage and supplies; yet, I did not have to pay the stations a membership fee until I tried to get on some big city stations. The responding stations wanted $100.00 or more for a yearly membership fee. There was no way I would have been able to afford to pay a membership fee in addition to the $125.00-$150.00 a month I was already spending out of my meager social security check to do the show. The only money I had tucked away was $100.00 left over from what an insurance company paid me to have my car fixed which I was saving toward having my book published. The Holy Spirit prodded my heart to use that money to pay a membership fee to a T.V station. I thought that what the Spirit was telling me was that the aforementioned station covered a city and 15 towns, and many more people would be reached with the gospel through that station than the number of people that would be reached with my book when it was published.

I contacted the station manager and had him send me a form to fill out; I did it in faith. The following evening at church one of the things my pastor stated during his message was that we should invest in the kingdom. I obeyed and God confirmed it.

CHAPTER 6

OUR HELPER

NICK OF TIME

One day I went to my housing complex office where I used to live to fill out a paper for the secretary. I wasn't sure what it was about except that it had to do with housing. I dutifully put my John Hancock on the line to which she pointed. As I was signing it I happened to say to her: "I thought this appointment was going to have something to do with the paper that I put in the slot in the lobby a couple of weeks ago."

"What paper", she asked. "The paper I needed you to fill out and sign for another government office". "That slot is only for rent checks. I never check that box until the first of the month". "Oh no", I replied, "The paper is dated and has to be returned within 15 days". "Oh no", she said. Simultaneously, we both started counting days on our fingers. "If you get it in the mail today they should receive it before the deadline in two days", she said as she hastily began to fill out the form which she had retrieved from the slot.

If the secretary had not called me to sign the housing paper that day, or if she had not called me until the following day, we would not have discovered that my papers were still in the rent box, and there was a big chance that I would have been denied assistance from the agency. Thank You, Father.

I would venture to say that God orchestrates happenings like this millions of times every week throughout the world; yet, the vast majority of people are so conditioned to chalk them up to happenstance that they fail to see an ever -loving God behind them.

PERFECT TIMING

On September 20, 2012 my youngest son was working on a fishing boat far out to sea when a terrible hurricane belted New England and the Atlantic Ocean. Try as he may, the captain was late in heading back to port which put the lives of his crew members at risk. My son called me from the satellite phone on the boat telling me of their concerns. I began to pray and put the prayer request out on Facebook. Within a short span of time I received another call telling me that they arrived in the harbor just 10 minutes before the authorities closed the hurricane barrier.

God is a God of perfect timing!

COMPUTERS: GOOD/BAD

My computer had been acting up for months. That little blue circle that tells us that the computer is thinking kept going round and round all the time. Although I took it into the shop and they kept it for four days and got rid of some viruses and malware, it still acted even worse when I got it home. I could not bring myself to take it back to the shop as I was behind in all my computer work, and in my mind it seemed that fighting with it at home at my desk was the lesser of two evils.

On one particular day, battling with the p.c. was especially trying. The malware detection link prevented me from accessing the Internet altogether. I knew I should have called the computer geeks, I chided myself, but I had electricians running through the house all that day; my online banking was completely messed up and I had been on the phone with the bank reps and supervisors for two hours; I was frazzled. I could not take on any more mental irritability.

That evening I decided to simply get away from my desk and to lie on my couch and watch a movie. As I lay there a very peaceful calm came over me, and I felt a slight nudging from the Holy Spirit of God telling me to go to my computer and to do exactly what He told me to do. His first prompt was for me to go to the control panel where programs could be uninstalled. I reminded God that I did not have any savvy about such things. He told me in my spirit to uninstall Google Chrome because Google Chrome was fighting against Mozilla Firefox which I also had installed on my computer and had never uninstalled. I followed His instructions.

To my delight and exhilaration my computer reverted to the original state it was in many months earlier and performed beautifully; I had my computer back!

Who, but God, could do something like that!

The following morning as I lay in bed, the thought came to me that the two programs Mozilla Firefox and Google Chrome could not inhabit the same computer. God brought to mind the Scriptures that tell us that we cannot serve two masters; Satan cannot cohabitate with the Holy Spirit.

COMPUTER SCARE

On July 9, 2012 a vast number of computers in the country were supposed to be infected with multiple viruses, plus the private information of computer owners was threatened to be compromised. I had no knowledge of the threats until I walked across the street to do laundry where I used to live and went to sit in the gazebo with my neighbors while my clothes were in the dryer. One person began talking about the threat, and informed the rest of us that at 12:01 a.m. the hackers would get in and do their damage. She warned us women that we should go online and check our computers, and if needed, we should fix them.

Not having enough computer savvy to handle anything that big on my own, I called the computer geeks at a large, national chain through which I have my protection program. I suspected that they were weary from being inundated with calls because I was given the run around. What was I to do? I prayed.

Seconds after I hung up from the geeks, my best friend, Linda, called and gave me the FBI website that all Americans were encouraged to go to in order to combat the computer threat. I was able to follow the instructions from home without taking the computer to the shop. I was a happy camper and immensely thankful to God for His help.

MY HOME PERM

After spending over $55.00 for a perm and $10.00 for a tip (and even more as prices went up) every three months for my whole life, I decided in the summer of 2012, due to my financial situation, that I would attempt to give myself a home permanent. I bought the necessary supplies at a local beauty supply store, and proceeded to place a sheet and some large towels on the floor along with a stand up mirror so that I could sit on the floor while undertaking the unpleasant task. My back condition hindered me from standing up to do it.

Applying the applicator and neutralizer and going through all the steps the first time went relatively well, although for some reason I didn't manage to get much curl. I figured it was because I only used half of the product being that my hair wasn't very long. Three months later when I again attempted the task, I ran into a problem that I had not faced the first time around. Because I used the ingredients more liberally, I had the activator and neutralizer dripping down my face like a water faucet. It was then that I realized that I had not purchased the long strand of cotton to wrap around my face for protection. Instantly my face began to burn. I grabbed a towel and began to blot my face. I didn't want to wash my whole head with clear water and abort the project as I was desperate to do something with my hair. Instead, I prayed and asked God to help me.

The thought came to me that a week prior when I was cleaning my bedroom closet, I came across some medicine cabinet items that I had stored away for nearly 10 years--items that I didn't have room for in my tiny bathroom. Included in the box of products was a bottle of aloe vera gel which I carried to my bathroom cabinet just in case I had a need for it.

The need for the aloe vera presented itself much sooner than I had expected--while perming my hair. I immediately flushed my eyes with water because they were burning and I was afraid of losing my sight. My cheeks continued to burn all the way to my eyes. So many things had gone viral in recent times regarding burns and steering the public away from old fashioned methods like applying butter and ice to burns, that I wasn't sure what to do until I prayed and God put the aloe vera on my mind. (He obviously orchestrated that I would find it just before I had a need for it.) I applied the soothing gel a few times during the rest of the process.

That evening and the following day, my face was red as rouge and rough as sandpaper. My skin had wrinkled slightly to my horror, yet I was so relieved that nothing had happened to my eyesight which was of greater concern to me. I continued to treat the burns and to apply moisturizer to my face, and within several days the blisters and roughness were gone.

Blessed be God Who is always near, and Who always comes to my rescue. I don't even want to think about what could have happened had He not intervened.

MY CAR WOULDN'T START

One morning when I was busy getting ready to move and I was heading out to get some cardboard boxes, my car wouldn't start. I had been paying my insurance company for emergency road protection for many years; yet, was unhappy with the way the company operated regarding road service. I figured the annoyance would become monumental as I started making phone calls. The company's plan required the driver to call a local road service place and to pay the bill and then they would reimburse me. I was never financially secure enough to do that. Well, this time was different. I called the branch of the insurance company that I switched over to whereby the secretary was quick to give me a direct phone number to road service which meant that I would not have to pay anything up front. After I called the number I was given a second number that I could call if need be. I was in disbelief! I was given not only one, but two direct phone numbers to road service.

Another cool thing that happened was that while I was sitting in the car waiting for the road service man to come, I decided that I would do some cleaning. I started with the glove compartment, the box next to the driver's seat and every compartment I could find. I came across seven bottles of nail polish, my original house key which I had been searching for and a lot more. Redemption.

The service person started the car simply by turning the key by what he called a fluke (?????). He said that I needed a new starter. He said I should leave it running because f I didn't it might not start again. I left it running for over a half hour, but it seemed ridiculous to me so I turned it off. I called my kids who told me that I probably needed to have the battery terminals cleaned. I took the car to a nearby car place to get the battery terminals cleaned for $14.95 explaining the problem to the mechanic there. He checked out the battery and starter and told me that there was no problem with the starter. The other mechanic performed another service having to do with protection costing $13.00. I was good to go. I went to pay them with my debit card for cleaning the terminals and they wouldn't take any money---said it was a freebee. That confirmed what I already knew that God would not allow the car to start on Tuesday in order to bring about some awesome blessings---getting the phone numbers which gave me indescribable security, finding the key that had been missing and to bring about the following testimony:

DIANA AND TOM

Because I couldn't drive to nearby stores to pick up some cardboard boxes for moving when my car wouldn't start, I posted at my Facebook site a request for boxes from anybody who lived in my area. The response was almost immediate. Two acquaintances that I had not seen in 25 years, Tom and Diana, happened to have some brand, new moving boxes in their garage and wondered if I would like them to bring them over. "Yes, that would be wonderful," I replied.

A couple of hours later they showed up with six brand new moving boxes which Diana assembled and taped up with sealer tape. They also brought with them a homemade treat for me, Diana's famous English toffee which she sells on the Internet. I never tasted such good candy.

We spent two hours reminiscing and sharing God's love and blessings. What a blessed time! ...all because my car wouldn't start.

SITUATION IN THE FAMILY

I can't say why I was getting paranoid one night because it was a private family matter, but my heart was as heavy as an anvil. I went to God's Word and he gave me a verse in the Psalms that read: "God, be my help in this hour of crisis". I thought it was such a beautiful verse. I put a prayer request on a prayer chain, 'a call to anguish', consisting of close friends. When I went to bed I repeated the verse over and over around 200 times. God, in His goodness, lifted the pressure from me. I was able to sleep all night long.

The following morning God reversed the desperate situation. That is what happens when we take His promises to heart and take Him at His Word.

MY BACK THANKS YOU

The second day of spring was upon us. I, being warm blooded, was too warm for comfort as I worked at my keyboard. I quickly changed my long-sleeved shirt for a short-sleeved one. While the armoire door was open, my eyes caught site of several of my winter sweat shirts and turtle necks. A fleeting thought went through my mind that I should bag them up for storage and pull out some of my summer clothes which were packed away in my storage area across the street from my apartment--- but---how would I handle a project as huge as that being that I was in so much back pain? I put my thoughts to rest not even praying about what I should do and continued with my typing.

A half hour later someone came knocking at my front door. My friend, Helen, smiled at me through the screen door. I had insisted that she swing by after she went to WalMart. She was way older than me, yet stronger than a horse. She was always asking what she could do to help me. I didn't think about the winter and summer clothes I wished to switch early on during her visit, but after a couple of hours I asked how she would feel about walking over to my storage area with me. She was happy to help out.

God had it all planned. He was my Helper.

HE GOT ME OUT OF IT

I did it again. I ran ahead of God and agreed to something because of sentimentality; I wanted to keep my business in the church Body. A certain businessman made an amazing impact on me and I thought I was acting in God's behalf to plan to hire him in the future.

Wrong...

When the time came for me to acquire information regarding my taking on a certain company, I plunged through the formalities even though I knew in my spirit that I was supposed to go with another businessman.

Oh boy. What have I done? It was nothing too major for God to handle though; that was for sure. After the man and I exchanged a few e-mails, he was led by God to suggest that I conduct my business with another company, a better fit for me. I'm sure he felt that his suggestion was in my best interest looking at the financial angle. I so appreciated his honesty and help, and I so appreciated God's intervention in my dealings.

CHAPTER 7

THOUGHTS

RUNNING THE RACE

Have you ever been to a football game or seen one on T.V. where one team was behind the second team by a mere couple of points, and then two seconds before the end of the game a runner from the losing team made a touchdown and scored points winning the game for his team? Have you watched the fans in the bleachers go ballistic? They waved banners like maniacs and hollered at the top of their lungs; they 'high-fived' every fan within their reach. The teammates on the field lifted the quarterback or whatever team member scored the touchdown to their shoulders and ran with him raised up for the crowd to see.

What about a horse race? Let's say the Kentucky Derby. One of the horses with its jockey is way behind going at a good pace; yet, other horses pass it by. By sight the two front runners are the only ones that stand a chance at crossing the finish line. Male fans puff on cigars while cheering for the horse on which they placed their bets. Women, their faces partially hidden under their broad -brimmed hats, scream- totally uninhibited- until they are hoarse. Then, just when it seems that all hope is gone for the horse which is the least favored to place, the thoroughbred picks up its gallop and ups its pace all the while the horses in the lead and those close behind start to wind down. The next thing you know the trailing horse starts passing all the rest of the horses one by one by one until it crosses the finish line and the crowd goes nuts.

That is the same exhilaration experienced by God's people called to be alive in our present, chosen generation in these last days of humankind. We await Christ's return with great anticipation. We grow to be like Him and we race toward the finish line.

THE STREAM

After I had lived in my last apartment for over a year I noticed that there was a very narrow stream passing through the woods in the vicinity of my back yard approximately 30 yards away. I noticed it one day when the bright sun shone on the water making it glisten. I had looked out my kitchen window at wild turkeys, birds of all kinds, beautiful white birches, squirrels, snow, more trees and always with an eye open for deer; yet, I never saw the beautiful stream so close by the back side of my house. I couldn't believe that I had never seen it before. It reminded me of how much beauty there is in nature and in God's kingdom here on earth; yet, so many people are blind to so many things. We go about our daily routines and get so caught up with our schedules that we miss the beautiful streams that are practically under our noses. God, please open thousands of eyes today just as You opened mine when I discovered the stream in my backyard.

DEEP LESSON

I learned an astounding lesson one time and it came about because of one of my former neighbors. The tenants where I lived at the time had assigned parking places, but it was casual, and if someone else or someone's company parked in any of our places it was no big deal…except for one neighbor. The woman's assigned parking place happened to be close to the entrance to my apartment. Because there were so few slots for guest parking, guests sometimes parked in the woman's assigned parking space. I started to hear stories about her blowing her horn and yelling at people right after I moved into the neighborhood. One neighbor said that her husband had died and the undertaker came to her house to conduct financial matters pertaining to her deceased husband's funeral when all of a sudden someone outside started blowing the horn on her car --non-stop. She looked out the window and discovered that the funeral director had parked his car in the space belonging to the disgruntled neighbor. Given the circumstances of his visit, she was embarrassed.

I wasn't added to the infuriated neighbor's list of enemies until after I lived there for a year. I knew that it was my responsibility to make sure that my visitors didn't park in her space, and I had gone out front in freezing, cold weather on many occasions to make sure that it did not happen; yet, things happen…like the time that my granddaughter came to visit. I was not paying attention to where she parked because I was videoing my little great-granddaughter, Aaliyah, as she ran from the car --pitter-patter, pitter-patter -- all excited calling Nana, Nana.

A short time later when the neighbor whose parking space my granddaughter Rachael parked in came home she landed on her horn 15 times. Aaliyah had been playing with her mother's car keys, and so it took a whole minute for her mom to find them in order to go outside to move her car. After she did so she acted courteously and waited for the woman to park and went up to the side of her car to apologize. The woman wasn't in the mood for any apologies; she was fuming. She yelled at my granddaughter telling her that it was my fault for allowing her to park there. I felt so bad for my granddaughter because she loves elderly people and is even studying to become an advocate for seniors.

A couple of days later I heard from some of the other neighbors that the horn blower was furious with me and hated me. I had gone to the woman's house on another occasion to try to apologize for the fact that she wasn't invited to an impromptu neighborhood barbeque that was held up in our section of housing, only to be told that she wasn't supposed to talk to me because I wasn't of the same religion as she. I was not going to be offering any more apologies any time soon especially when she was the one who aggravated the situation. In fact, I was so upset at how she treated my granddaughter that I tried to get the management to force the woman to write a letter of apology to my granddaughter, but it didn't happen.

The scenario repeated itself when the lady who vacuumed for me absent-mindedly parked in my across the street neighbor's parking spot one morning. I tried to meet the cleaning woman at her designated time of arrival to make sure she didn't park there, but she came 45 minutes late so what was I supposed to do---wait at the door for all that time? I simply left my front door ajar and went to the back of the house to start working on my computer. The cleaning lady let herself in, and was vacuuming and did not hear the neighbor's horn blowing until she turned off the vacuum cleaner. She came into my bedroom to tell me that she had to go outside to move her car. Another neighbor called on the phone to tell me that our enraged neighbor beeped the horn 18 times.

When the first incident happened I became upset for a time and had to repent and ask for God's forgiveness. I did not want to harbor any bad feelings toward anyone; therefore, when the second incident happened I wasn't fazed. I stood fast in the love of God and would not be swayed by anybody. I even prayed for the woman. Just minutes after I prayed for her, parenthetically, God gave me this verse (wait till you hear it): Proverbs 14:21, "He who despises his neighbor sins against God, his fellowman and himself". I am so glad that He gave me that verse after I prayed for her and not before; yea for me.

Just before I read that verse I read something that read: Don't only grasp the Bible in your head--let it go to your heart. And I also read in an old, old version of the Bible another verse that grabbed me: "Let us not give ourselves the liberty of disputing with the wicked and sinners lest we should chance in time to become like them". I purposed to adhere to the verse about not despising one's neighbor. Not that I despised the neighbor who was unkind to me and my family; I had to purpose to get rid of negative feelings. The Holy Spirit was doing His job of keeping me in check and keeping me pure; it was up to me to do my part.

THE LIVING WORD

Imagine that you are a student at a school. It could be in an elementary school, high school or college. Imagine that the teacher passes out books and asks all the students to begin reading. You start at the first page and realize that the book has to do with you. From page to page, paragraph to paragraph and sentence to sentence the words pertain to your life in one way or another. The words actually speak to you regarding your heart and soul, your likes and dislikes, your frailties and flaws, your good points, your character, your passions, your spirituality, your relationships with family and friends. The book reveals itself like the imaginary friend you had as a young person; the one with whom you shared everything. The thing of it is that it is not weird or scary, but rather sweet, pleasant, wonderful and euphoric.

The other students in the class are having the exact same experience with their books. The covers of their books are the same as yours, and many of the pages are filled with the same content, but the words are directed to each one differently according to who they are and where they are at spiritually, mentally and emotionally. The class is spellbound as the books have a hold on the group as a whole as well as on each one, individually.

You turn one page after the other trying anxiously to digest the credulous amount of information about your secret being .The more you read the more connected you are to the One Who wrote the Book. The more you start to realize that it is more about Him than it is about you; your Spirits begin to mesh. This Person is a Being; He is Love. Your whole person is consumed with love. Your soul is deeply impacted even before you get to the end of the Book.

The Book is a Book of life. It may be written in thousands of languages, but spiritually it is written in just one language….God's language. The word is alive; it is true; it is the Bible. It contains 66 love letters written by the Holy Spirit of God and penned by men of God for you.

GIVING

When we give offerings to others in our hardship is when we truly get financially blessed. We are not supposed to wait until we have money left over to give to God. We should give to God from off the top. It is always a blessing for me to practice this. Of course, I must keep these things secret, but just to give some readers an idea of what I mean I'll share this one little episode. A missionary friend visited my church service. I didn't have enough to eat here in the states, yet I knew I had much more than he so I walked up to him and handed him a roll of quarters. The quarters were half of my monthly laundry money, and being on a tight budget I figured that I would end up washing some clothes by hand, but that would glorify God to the 'umpth' degree, not to mention that I would get blessed for it.

Two days after I gave away the roll of quarters, and 20 minutes after I wrote the above story, I was informed by one of my T.V. stations that I would not have to pay the yearly membership fee of $125.00 to have my shows aired on that station as I thought I would have to pay; I was speechless!)

INSIGHTS

God gave me four insights in one day --- verses that were illuminated like never before even though I had read them many times before.

Insights #1and #2… Solomon entered into counsel with his mind. Ecclesiastis 1:16...and then I read in Ecclesiastis 2:1: "I said in my mind". These two verses depict that God's Spirit meets our spirit in our minds, and that we should 'on purpose' enter into counsel with our minds.

#3… 1 Samuel 9:15: "The Lord had revealed to Samuel in his ear…" Now why do you suppose that it was written that way? Why wasn't it written---'the Lord revealed to Samuel---?' Why does it say: "the Lord revealed to Samuel in his ear?" I think it is because God wanted to point out to Bible readers that we should listen intently with our ears.

#4... 1 Samuel 9:26, "Saul stayed overnight at Samuel's house. Samuel woke Saul in the morning". I was somewhat troubled with reading that. If I stayed overnight with a prophet of God, I certainly would be up before he got up in the morning. I would be waiting to glean from him. I think it brings out Saul's character. We all know what kind of man Saul was, but this verse confirms what we already know.

FOCUSING OUR THOUGHTS

We are living in a day when many Christians are victoriously finishing their courses. However, at times believers will not complete God's call or a specific job that they have started because they won't receive God's grace to finish; when tests come they quit. Many put their hand to the plow, but take steps backwards as the pressures of this life come against their spiritual progress.

God showed me that some of the areas of which the saints don't seem to be cognizant are as follows: Christians often do not forsake unrighteous thoughts. They don't 'on purpose' think what God thinks or allow Him to possess their minds. Christians should repent of ungodly thoughts. Jesus taught the disciples to pray, "lead us not into temptation" (Matthew 6:13a), so they would not be overcome by the pressures of trials and testings that they faced each day. Do we pray not to be lead into temptation? We must not get lax when it comes to praying in specifics.

A GOOD SAYING

GOD IS NOT BEATING YOU UP WITH HIS TEACHING, HE IS SAVING YOU ....

PROSPERITY AND ADVERSITY

I was lying in bed early one morning thinking about how difficult it is for human beings to live on this earth with so many demons manifested in the atmosphere. I felt bad that so many of my fellowmen were not able to deal with life and its problems. I thought about the large numbers of them who are caught up in hard-heartedness concerning the gospel message, and wondered why they would have to go to hell when they never asked to be born. I am glad that God stopped me in my tracks before I got carried away further; that is such a ploy of the devil. He wants people to think that God is sadistically cruel and heartless; yet, the opposite is true; God has a heart. His heart is so colossal, so beautiful and so loving that He sent His only Son to die for us. He sent Him to be a ransom for us. How does a person conclude that God is a sadist from that! It is totally ludicrous!

I thought about the days of the cavemen. Comparing our present time with those times, we have a great deal for which to be thankful. And then I meditated about the days when battles were going on continually the way it has been in Israel. What must it be like for parents to be afraid to send their children to the park? I reflected on how it would be if humans lived in an environment which lacked the love of God, with cold-heartedness permeating the air, running rampant. I imagined that humans would simply exist and not live. And then I sensed that an infinite God had all this in mind before He made plans for the earth and its inhabitants.

God did not slap me down for wondering about some of these things; contrarily, He answered me within a few minutes during my a.m. devotional in His Word. He graciously led me to Ecclesiastes 7:14, '....God has made prosperity side by side with adversity so that man may not find out anything that shall be after him.' The first part of the verse, 'He made one side by side with the other,' spoke volumes to me and went along with my thoughts about good and evil.

WHO IS THIS GOD?

When you can't take life for another minute often something happens that is totally unexpected and keeps you from cracking up. How many times have you said: 'I can't take it for another minute?' From my observations when people get that low, God often reveals Himself in unique ways through other people. It is during those times that we are so utterly blown away that all we could ask is: Who is this God?

GOD'S COMPASSION FOR FRIENDS

I have witnessed God's compassion for people hundreds of times and been repeatedly blessed by His deep caring. Witnessing these events never gets old. I have watched women who have come to my house pour out their heart and soul, and sensed that the Holy Spirit compassion coming from my heart was God's and God's, alone. I have watched emotional healings take place and sensed that scars were erased. I have been awed at how the God of the universe, almighty God, could come down in the midst of me and whomever I am with to perform healings that are completely divine.

ABSORBED ADMIRATION

Someone who was at the end of herself came to see me. She had been holding onto something for years. She poured it all out as if it came from a water faucet. Although she had brought her problems on herself because of going against God's Word, He was not insensitive to the pressure she was under. He, instead, smothered her with His absorbed admiration which is what she so desperately needed, and that is how He started a healing process in her soul.

THE ANSWER IS YES

The answer is yes. The question is: Do I ever question God? But...the questions are short-lived because I know I am not supposed to question God. The squirming requests may wiggle their way through my thoughts in an unsuspecting, fleeting sort of way from time to time; yet, I try to the point of exasperation to give no mind to the ignominious creatures. God, Who knows that my intentions are pure, sometimes chooses to respond to the questions even though I am perfectly contented without knowing the answers one way or the other.

The enemy is always slamming criticisms and accusations at my mind. That is why it is imperative for me and everyone else to armor our minds with divine protection in the early morning. For instance--when I record all these testimonies and thoughts to pass on, he sends an impulse that communicates to me that nobody but nobody is going to give a darn about these insignificant, old lady stories and why am I even wasting my time? Trust me--I could go on and on and on and on and on... The Holy Spirit instantly retaliates with the thought that whatever I do following the leading of the Holy Spirit I do as according to Him. What He does with it is His business, not mine. I must remove myself from all of it; I am just an instrument, a vessel. I am not the author; He is.

DAVID, DAVID, DAVID!!!!

Long ago, when I read the story about King David's son, Amnon, raping his half sister Tamar, it left me mildly upset with King David. I may be pretty naive sometimes and lack discernment sometimes, but I cannot imagine myself falling for the malarkey that Amnon gave David about not being able to get well unless his sister was allowed to prepare some cakes and to serve them to him. Give me a break already.

Just because of Amnon's deception, an innocent, young girl suffered severe emotional repercussions for a long period of time. And because of his evil deed his brother, Absalom, was tormented with hatred for

Amnon for two long years which resulted in him having his brother killed. It is all pretty difficult to digest.

I guess there are things that I do that would irritate King David, as well, if he were alive and knew me. Just sayin…

IN A RUT

Many have heard me compare one's refusal to take advantage of the freedom that we were given in Christ, Jesus to chickens tied together in a crate to be transported to market, and being untied when they get there and given the chance to free themselves from their circumstances and to walk around; yet, they do not because they are afraid to move. I have been thinking even harder about it and this illustration came to mind: I think it was in the year 2006 when my printer started giving me grief. It would print, but if I was not right next to it to catch each paper that had finished printing, the printer would eat up the paper. My son Gary had a printer that he wasn't using and he gave it to me. It was not the same make as mine, and because I can't stand change or adapting to something new, I decided that I did not want it and tried to give it back to him. He did not want it back.

So, here is the rest of the story: I put Gary's printer under my bed and each time I moved to a different apartment I would put the newer printer under my bed. For seven years each time that I have printed something (which amounts to several hundreds of times,) I stay right in front of my old printer to catch each paper when it is finished printing. If someone happens to knock on my door before the paper is finished printing, depending on whether it is at the beginning or end of the paper, I either holler out for them to wait a minute or I make a mad dash to the front door and back to my desk in order to catch the paper being printed before it gets eaten up.

I know it sounds stupid and ridiculous, and it is stupid and ridiculous, but I am stuck there and because of my stubbornness I can understand some peoples' mentality in staying stuck in their bondage in not allowing

Christ's freedom to rule in their lives; it is the same principle; we are creatures of habit.

NO STONES

Please do not throw stones at me for writing this, but regarding the bombings on American soil becoming more frequent, do you think it could be possible that they are an answer to the millions of prayers for revival in America i.e...Christians pray and ask God for revival. Adversity and affliction are needed for the lost to come to their knees, and for some Christians to get out of their lackadaisical places and to go on with Christ. Could God be allowing the bombings and terrible happenings to bring about millions of salvations? Just asking...

THOSE NOISY SEAGULLS

For a year and a half at my old apartment I was awakened before five every morning by the loud cawing of birds which I assumed were crows. I would tell my neighbors who lived at the farther end of the complex about them all the time reminding them how lucky they were not to have been awakened by the unpleasant noises each day. Then one day I awoke when it was still dark and sauntered into my living room to open my blinds, and what did I see, but the street in front of my apartment filled with seagulls. They were standing completely still on the street appearing as a blanket of snow in a scene from a winter wonderland, yet it was in the month of April and spring- like.

All the time I thought it was the crows that were driving me crazy; it was not, it was the seagulls. So what is the big deal about this you may wonder? The big deal is that every time my thinking is off (case in point-crows vs seagulls,) God wants me to know that my thinking is off no matter how trivial it may seem, and for that I thank Him.

JEALOUSY

This is not simply a thought or something I made up; my head pastor shared it from the pulpit. It makes sense and I believe it. Jealousy produces stomach pain. In a study I did one time on the human body I delved into how it reacts to different emotions. I think my pastor's message was a confirmation from God having to do with my study.

Stop and think about how jealousy tears you up especially if another person comes between you and the person with whom you are in a relationship. It destroys; it consumes; it steals your happiness, your sanity, your stability. Imagine the turmoil that goes on in the brain. If a computer could generate a video of the inside of a person's head, and liken it to a computer game of space wars, that would present a clear picture of what happens to men and women when their spouses cheat; of what happens when someone is jealous of another's promotion; of what happens when one person is jealous of another's looks and the list goes on. Those debilitating mind functions travel all the way to the stomach and cause all the body parts near the stomach to malfunction producing pain.

Jealousy, according to the Bible, is as cruel as the grave. In writing this I see that there is only one letter difference in grave and grace. In considering a variety of subjects as well as jealousy, we can choose between the grave or grace--grave meaning death to a situation, or grace meaning what God wants to give us to walk through it without being harmed.

CHAPTER 8

LESSONS

THE OSCARS

Someone who was being interviewed on the red carpet at the Oscar's one year said this: "It is such a strange feeling to be playing a part and having the make-up artists change your appearance, and then to look in a mirror and see someone else, yet you know it's really you inside that body." I got to thinking---it is the same with us as Christians. We have Jesus living inside of us; yet, we see our earthly selves as we look into a mirror. This was really heavy to meditate on; yet, it gave me a new perspective. A day or two later I went to T.J. Maxx to check out their clearance sales and to buy a bra. When I was in the fitting room trying it on, I could not help but go into shock to see my form in the mirrors lined up on three different sides of the small room. The brightness was nearly blinding from the florescent lighting. Believe me, nothing was hidden; the poor state of my nakedness was exposed. It was the first time in a long time that I was able to see what my back looked like from my left side where most of my disproportion is located. I was in total shock! The shape of my back was disgustingly deformed and disfigured. I could hardly believe my eyes. The security guy who is a stationary fixture above the fitting room ceiling had to be in shock as well…(yes, you read this right.)

On the way home many thoughts went through my head. What would become of me in the years ahead? I suspected that I was on the threshold of immovability. I wondered if I would end up in a nursing home, or if I would have to embark on taking in a full time nursing assistant to come to my house. I wondered if I would become permanently bedridden. I didn't verbalize my thoughts to God, but I was doing a lot of thinking.

 When I arrived home I went directly to my Bible to seek out God. He gave me portions of Scripture to address my dilemma: The first was from the Book of Job where He admonished me not to question Him concerning the shape in which He made me. The second was in the Book of Ezekiel where the question was posed, "Why did you make me this shape?" And I'm pretty certain this next one came from the Book of Jeremiah, "The pot has no right to say to the potter-- why did you make me this shape?"

 I may not have verbalized my thoughts to God; yet, He knew my thoughts and answered me dead-on. I was tongue-tied.

SPEECH CONSCIOUS

One day the Lord spoke to me about our language. The next day He gave me these verses to coincide with what He had given me the day before.

Zephaniah 3:9, "…for then (changing their impure language.) I will give to the people a clear and pure speech from pure lips, that they may all call upon the name of the Lord. To serve Him with one, unanimous consent and one united shoulder bearing the yoke of the Lord".

Zephaniah 3:12, "…neither shall a deceitful tongue be found in their mouth".

Try as I may I occasionally slip an ungodly, unfeminine word into my conversation. God hears every syllable that comes out of my mouth, and He checks me on what does not line up with His character. I used the word 'screw' and was immediately convicted and I repented. I did not expect such intense disciplinary action, but it came. The following morning the Holy Spirit gave me 1 Tim 6:20, "O timothy, guard and keep the deposit entrusted to you. Turn away from the irreverent babble and godless chatter, with the vain and empty and worldly phrases, and the subtleties and the contradictions in what is falsely called knowledge and spiritual illumination".

MORE SPEECH CONSCIOUSNESS

Careful not to say any unkind things about the Body of Christ…

Careful not to be careless and promote atonement…

GIVING IN HARDSHIP

Giving in our hardship tremendously blesses God. Every time I give in my hardship it is not as if I say to myself, "No problem, I'll get back double". Believe me; it's not like that; it's like getting a knife in my chest. It takes me a half a year to put just a few hundred dollars away for a big project, and that fund is the only place from which I can borrow for gifts etc. My dwindling fund gnaws at me incessantly, yet God always gives it back and more besides. When He does give it back I am not nonchalant about His giving it back. I am swept away with surprise as if it is the first time God has ever done it.

JUST A THOUGHT

If I could relive my youth I would dress in my cheerleader's outfit and get some pom- poms and get in the middle of a football field and lead the fans into cheers for our wonderful, almighty King Jesus.

THOMAS JEFFERSON

I have listened to recordable books about Thomas Jefferson, and, like others, have wrongly judged him for fathering a child by his servant girl, Sally. However, when I watched a documentary, 'A View From The Mountain', in which the whole story was brought out about the young girl, I chided myself for judging Mr. Jefferson. Sally Hemings was the daughter of his full time housekeeper Betty Hemings. Sally's father was Thomas Jefferson's father-in-law, his deceased wife Martha's father. Sally was three -quarters white. The documentary brought out that more than likely Sally had a keen resemblance to Mr. Jefferson's wife, Martha, whom he cherished, and that is probably what attracted him to her. He took her to France with him, and considering the time factor, that is where she conceived their child, Thomas.

Sally Hemings gave birth to three or four more children by at least two more men---probably men of means. It is disparaging to jump to conclusions about things that are not our business. We think we know it all, but we don't. Thank You, Lord, for setting me straight!

PRINCESS DI

Years after the death of Princess Diana I watched a movie which depicted that she was murdered. The assemblage of facts, the police report and all findings presented are said to be factual. I am convinced that the details were not fraudulently represented. One cannot watch the movie without reaching a similar conclusion, I believe. A New York reporter, Rachael (I can't remember her last name) was on assignment in Paris, France to cover Princess Diana's arrival there. She was one of the first reporters to hear of Diana's pregnancy which the princess was planning to announce publicly within days.

Rachael was given a heads up about aspects going amiss, and along with her French policeman friend, raced on a motorcycle to try to ward off a death plot on Diana following the paparazzi and the persons allegedly responsible for the fatal accident in which Diana and her fiancé were killed. She witnessed the removal of pertinent evidence from the scene by the police; noted that incriminating evidence was omitted from the police reports, and was an eyewitness that the whole truth about the accident was covered up.

Rachael's room at the Ritz Hotel in Paris was broken into and her laptop and numerous items were stolen, along with any correspondence she had with her newspaper office in New York City. All evidence of what really happened was missing. Her policeman friend who conspired with her was killed, and an attempt was made on her life which left her with multiple, broken bones and confined to a hospital for a lengthy stay, yet she survived.

This story may not seem like it belongs in this book, yet I considered it to be a lesson. It is so easy to jump on the bandwagon and believe what everybody else believes; yet, we should always investigate matters further before coming to any conclusions. We may discover that the truth is different than what is publicized by the media.

ON VACATION

One summer when I took my second of two camping trips, my only two 'get-aways' in years, I dreamed of catching up on reading and of drinking in the alluring outdoors. Separating from everything that was familiar; from everything that was pressing, and breathing in change in a placid environment welcomed high spirits. Nobody could demand my time. Wrong. I must have forgotten momentarily that I was called to be one of God's messengers and not a free agent. In the Book of Isaiah we read that He is present with us no matter where we are. He not only saw me sitting in my cabin; He placed me there. And He sent others there to me. People came knocking at the oddest times in the most unusual of circumstances. When I heard the first knock just seconds after I sat down with my book, I remember grumbling to myself and saying to the Lord, "I do not appreciate Your humor". I spontaneously heard the voice of the Holy Spirit say to me, 'It is not about you; it is about Me'. So I put off

the old and put on the new according to the Word of God and ended up
ministering Christ, counseling, pouring out God's wisdom and advice
and being available to Him even on my vacation.

A GOOD ONE

1 Corinthians 3:9, "We are laborers with Him--His husbandry--His
building--His farm--His architecture--His structure…He is the architect
and we are His master builders (from my head pastor.)

HE DOES WHAT HE HAS TO

Has anyone ever heard of taking a day off from prayer? Well, I think I
invented it one day. It was a busy Saturday and I had a concert scheduled
for that evening. I prayed early that morning (ritualistically,) but I did not
cover my mind in prayer the way I had usually done because I was busy
with other things. I should have known that I was vulnerable for ambush
from the devil because something had been plaguing me for two weeks.
Instead of taking it to God in prayer, I allowed it to escalate. Before I
even realized it I found myself telling a friend about it. I guess I was
pretty cocky because I was planning to sing that night, and I never
considered the consequences of denying Christ and trying to minister in
song without confessing my iniquity.

I remember silently saying to the Lord that I felt ashamed for gossiping
and He needed to do what He needed to do to get my attention. He
heeded me. I got up to sing a song that would have been extremely
appropriate for the Easter season. The fellow operating the sound system
put in my C.D. The song, which I had practiced with no problem earlier
in the day, would not play; it kept jumping from song #1 to song #4 by -
passing my selection. It took several minutes for the sound man to find
my second selection which I barely made it through without any practice.
I was embodied in a web of embarrassment and humiliation. I thought
the song would never end; it was the worst of the worst. I am certain that

the listeners were blessed, and that I was being unduly hard on myself; yet, we all know that we know when God is trying to get our attention. I instinctively knew Who was behind the C.D. going berserk. I was glad the C.D. went berserk. God did not deserve what I had done to Him. I was given the privilege of bringing peoples' hearts to Him in appreciation for what He did on the cross, and, what did I do? I botched it up.

Like with the Apostle Peter and his sanguine temperament, mine displayed its ugly self, and I became ridden with a monsoon of guilt feelings and shame. I knew I had to go to the Word when I got home, but I trembled at having to do so. These are the words I read: "…those whom I love have turned against me". Slam…I closed the Bible as those words pierced my heart. I repented. If I had my way I would have wallowed in those muddy waters; would have refused to give myself grace and to rebound; I deserved to bask in self hatred; but, I did not want my Lord to have to watch me in that condition so I asked for His help in forgiving myself.

If anyone ever hears me voice ungodly opinions just to let off steam, please do me a favor and slap me side the head.

Father, help me to saturate and fill my soul with Your Word even on my busiest of days--especially on my busiest of days.

THE PARTY

I was nervous about going to a family gathering and dwelled on it for weeks. The morning of the gathering arrived and I went to church where I asked my pastor's wife to keep me in prayer that afternoon. As soon as the service started we watched a five minute video of our founding pastor teaching a class in the late 80's. In it he stated: Why pray for peace? Why pray for forgiveness, strength, power or any of those? We already have these things, and all we have to do is to put them on. Are you afraid to go someplace? God will go with you. Wow---he was speaking right to me.

When I left church I told the pastor's wife that I didn't need her to pray. I was going to put on strength and power and go to the gathering with God. And I did. I simply performed the mental exercise of clothing myself with the Holy Spirit; putting a smile on my face; putting on confidence and strength and walking in grace. I ruled. It went exceedingly well.

CHAPTER 9

GOD'S PROVISIONS

MONEY AND SUPPLIES

Nobody knows but God what a hardship it is for me to purchase supplies for my public access T.V. show, and to almost single-handedly support the United Sates Post Office with the money it costs me each month to mail the D.V.D.'s to respective stations. He may not have dropped any money out of the sky when He chose to bless me one month, yet bless me He did.

My friend Ellie came to visit bringing with her a big box of mailing supplies and stamps from her husband's office one day. Her husband also gave her $40 in cash to give me, and I never met the man! Wow! So you see---when God calls you to do something He supplies your needs.

FREE NEWSPAPERS

My neighbor and I were taking a walk down to the end of our development one afternoon and noticed a bicycle right in the middle of the sidewalk. The young man who delivered newspapers to our complex was sitting in a nearby gazebo. We walked up to sit in the gazebo, as well. He appeared to be very unhappy about something. We exchanged small talk and then He told us that the newspaper delivery was way behind schedule. The weather was extremely hot and unbearably humid. He was getting more edgy by the minute as he waited for the newspapers to be delivered to him. I offered to let him use my cell phone to make a call.

He was a chatty, young person and the three of us chatted for close to an hour. He was bummed out about what was happening to our country, and felt hopeless as far as his future was concerned. He spoke of local government projects of which he was opposed. It was most impressive to speak with a young person who held down a part time job at a local business; operated a newspaper route and was more than mildly politically -minded.

During the course of our conversation he related to me that he was given four extra copies of the newspaper each day to give out to potential, new customers. He said he would be glad to give me one, an offer I quickly accepted. I explained to him where I lived in the complex. An hour or so later I heard someone fiddling with my screen door. I hurried from my bedroom to the front door just in time to see him before he rode away. "Thank you", I hollered, as I noticed a free copy of the newspaper stuck in the door. "You're welcome", he replied. "I'm going to adopt you", he added. "I'm going to adopt you too", I replied. "Would you like a bottle of cold water? It's awfully hot and humid". "I'd love one", he answered. I grabbed a bottle of water and a miniature chocolate bar from the refrigerator and took it to him. He drank some of the water and wiped the sweat from his brow, then ate the chocolate as he threw his leg over his bicycle seat and started to ride away. "Umm---this is good", he hollered.

Why do I have this story included in a chapter on God's provisions you may wonder? Well, I knew I would be moving within a year's time, and I didn't subscribe to any newspaper so I was already wondering what I would use to wrap all my breakable belongings. My new, young friend delivered a free paper to me for 6-8 weeks. I had all the paper I needed. God supplied.

GIFTS

I wish I had thought of recording all the gifts I have received over the years. I truly have the most generous of family and friends ever. My kids have taken me out for breakfast, lunch and dinner countless times. They have also given me money in several denominations. When I lived near them and I needed something done around my apartment, my second son would send one of his employees over to tackle the job. If I needed something done to my car, he took care of it. All my sons made all the holidays special for me along with stopping over to see me. My third son and his wife would stop by occasionally when they went to the Wal-Mart and were in my area. They will never know what a blessing their impromptu visits meant to me. Number four son, being unmarried, engages in conversation with me for hours. We cover almost every subject under the sun. Number one son wishes he could be available more, but I live too far away from him. My gratitude also goes out to my kids for the packages of meat they bring me when they are successful enough to kill a deer during hunting season, and fresh fish they bring me when they either catch fish or buy extra. I have a grateful heart.

Several of my visitors bring me journals. I guess it is because I am a writer. One friend once brought me a pen with a cross on top that lit up. I have had flowers and chocolates sent to me; been given jewelry, clothing, an array of beautiful scarves hand-made by my sister, books and booklets, free tickets and lots more.

It is always fun to receive gifts. God bless all of them for their giving hearts.

BRUTAL TEMPS

1-23-2013…the temp was below zero with a wind chill factor that was much lower. My girlfriend was supposed to come over, but she didn't dare leave her house. I wanted so badly to go to the post office because my daughter-in-law had a birthday coming up and she and my son were headed to Florida in a few days, and I wanted her birthday card to arrive at their house before they left. Also, I had videoed my friend, Pastor Colby's, birthday party three days before, putting the video on a D.V.D' for him, and knew he would love to get it in the mail. I ran out of stamps though and there was no way that I would venture out in such frigid temperatures; I wouldn't even walk to the mailbox across the street.

That morning as I worked at my desk I noticed on my housing, community calendar that my neighbor Sheri was having a birthday that day. I called her to wish her a Happy Birthday although she wasn't home. I had to leave her a message on her voice mail. An hour or so later Sheri called me to thank me for the birthday call and wish even though it wasn't actually her birthday that day. "Today isn't my birthday", she said, "it isn't until next week, the 30th. The person who typed up the newsletter listed my birthday as the 23rd by mistake". After talking about the weather, and after mentioning that I wasn't going to make it to the post office, she asked if she could mail anything for me or get my mail from my mail receptacle. I didn't want her to have to go out into the cold so I turned down her offer. The wonderful, giving person that Sheri is, she wouldn't take no for an answer insisting on coming over to get my parcels and on bringing stamps over with her. Sheri put all my parcels into the mail slot for the mailman to take when he came. It was so good to get that off my mind. I took a deep, relaxing breath.

The way I see it is that God had the person who wrote the newsletter write down the wrong birth date for Sheri so that I would be in touch with her on the day of the frigid temperatures, putting her in a position to offer to mail my parcels for me saving me from going out in sub zero temperatures.

Ya gotta love His ways…

CENTRAL AIR

I have never thought that in my lifetime, I, like people who are financially comfortable, would enjoy the luxury of central air conditioning, yet in April of 2013 it was announced to the residents of my Brunswick, Maine complex that we would have central air plus a new heating system installed. God was the only One Who knew that my window air conditioner was on the fritz. And to think that I almost bought an indoor a/c unit the preceding year! Thank You, Lord, for preventing me from charging a stand up air conditioner, and thank You for Your wonderful provision.

THEY KEEP COMING

Even as I am writing this chapter the gifts keep coming. I just went to the mailbox, and what do you think was in it? A gift! My friends Bud and Christine from Florida sent me two bracelets and one ankle bracelet that Bud bought while in Cuba donating his services to help build a hospital there. Can you imagine them thinking of me because of the time that I spent on the island, and making sure they had the opportunity to bless me?

CAMPING TRIP 2013

I hoped that I would be able to return to the cottage on Damariscotta Lake in Maine in 2013, the year after I spent two separate vacations there. The thoughts of the lake, nature with all the wildlife especially the distinct species of birds and a kaleidoscope of vibrant colors began to tantalize my mind. All that I had to do was to close my eyes and to block out everything, and I could imagine myself inside the screened -in house at the water's edge on my chaise lounge chair with a good book and a glass of iced tea.

My back would not allow me the pleasure, however. Camping, even in a cottage, would involve a fair amount of packing, much more than I would be able to tackle. I began to entertain the blues until my old, camping neighbors, Steve and Rhonda, whom I had met at the campground the year earlier, invited me to come and stay with them at the cottage they were renting on the lake. What a provision from God! I thought it was majorly selfless of them for who would want to share their vacation time and space with a third person?

With just a minimum of things to pack, I planned my get-away. I had moved from one apartment to another and after all the packing and unpacking and changing addresses and the whole nine yards, I was tired. The thoughts of having two free days filled with me with great anticipation.

The end of July was on my doorstep. I headed north to the campground. It was wonderful meeting up with the Kinney's again and sharing meals. I even had my own room. I marvel at all the information I learn when I get together with other Christians. Sharing testimonies, especially, always broadens my horizons, and when I am with this couple there is an oasis of blessings from which to draw.

It poured cats and dogs the whole two days I was at the cottage with my friends. We couldn't go swimming or take a walk or roast marshmallows around a campfire at night—nada. But...our time together was so rich that we honestly and truly did not miss any of those things.

CHAPTER 10

OPPORTUNITIES

HOW DO I FORGIVE MYSELF?

A man I know e-mailed me early one morning to ask, "How do I forgive myself?" I stopped everything I was doing to answer him with the thoughts God put on my mind that very moment. They were so powerful that to file them or delete them would have been a shame so I am sharing them with all of you who read this book:

My response: 'I will tell you this from my personal experience. My past continues to haunt me now and then even at my age. I never took a drug in my life and I never slept around, but I did do some things that were unforgivable, so unforgivable as to haunt me. I guess that as long as the devil is alive and active it won't stop. What God has had me to do, and it has been more effective in my life in the last year, is to pray to have my faith increased. I need faith to believe that I am forgiven. When I buy into the devil's accusations, it means that I don't believe God for what the Bible says--plain and simple--so, when I ask for more faith (quality, not quantity) I believe that my sins have been buried in the deepest, deepest sea and that God has forgotten them. And why would I want to resurrect any sins that God has forgotten!!! The more we do this when the devil and his demons accuse us, the more it takes effect in our soul. Another thing I do is that when I pray every morning, I, on purpose, take off the old and put on the new (figuratively speaking) according to the Scriptures, and I ask God to cover my mind with the Blood of Jesus. The Blood is the only thing on this earth that Satan cannot penetrate. The more I do this the less the attacks come. I have to be faithful in doing it though.

I would suggest that you get to know the Apostle Paul. He did horrible things before God called him to be an apostle. He was a murderer; his heart was filled with venom. His heart did not always align with his actions, however; he was a thinker, and that may be the reason that God called him into the ministry. Because he responded to God's call straightaway; because he was steadfast in his new beliefs, and because he focused on God every, single day and didn't give in to the enemy, he became the greatest apostle that ever lived. That doesn't mean to say though that he NEVER EVER caved--he did. We don't know how many times he fell and had to get back up again when he was alone for three years being taught by God. We do know that when he was pretty despondent God sent Titus and others to strengthen him. So, growing in the Lord is a process.

So face each day as one day in the Lord's plan for your life. Don't look toward next week or next month. Ask for a double portion of grace to get you through. Get into the habit of praying for divine opportunities to help others even with something seemingly small like a word of kindness, for instance. The more we give out, the more we get back in the form of Jesus' character grafted into our character. The more time we spend with Him, the more love and mercy is poured into our lives.

So from now on when you look in the mirror tell yourself that you are a mirror of God's Son--that is how He sees you. You are no less than any pastor or evangelist or Body member. Write a sign that reads: "I AM NOT MY PAST' and put it on your refrigerator. I just spoke on that on my last show, 'Memories,'....check it out on my FB site or YOU TUBE. Every time you build yourself up you will combat the enemy. He will eventually get tired of you not reacting to him and he will move on. God loves you so much that He sent His Son to die for 'you'. He is with you and inside of you every minute of the day. You are one in Spirit with Him.

READER'S DIGEST FORMAT

Many relatives and friends have told me that they leave my book on their bedside tables and read one story a night before going to sleep. They say that the stories help them to relax. Others say that the stories are so compelling to read that they can't put the book down after reading one story; reading it is like trying to eat one Lay's potato chip. Whichever way suits your fancy, I just pray that each reader is blessed.

AWESOME OPPORTUNITY

For quite a while I had been praying for an opportunity to talk with the daughter of an acquaintance so that she could get to know me. From what I had heard she was totally against anyone who is born -again and hates any mention of God. That is so true of so many people. They label us as religious freaks; they judge us wrongly.

Well, I was sitting at a picnic table at a small ice cream shack one summer evening after supper savoring a mouthful of Maine's delicious Gifford ice cream--black cherry (if I remember correctly) when the daughter of my acquaintance with her son and daughter sat down right next to me. She proceeded to tell me that she watched my T.V. shows sometimes and enjoyed them; that to me was an answer to my prayers. Any exposure to the gospel will give God an opportunity to work in someone's heart; God is faithful in the small things.

From that conversation we went from one subject to another for almost an hour and a half. She really had the chance to see what I was about and that I was a regular woman; a mother, grandmother, sister and friend. She could see that I wasn't hyper- spiritual. We shared experiences that we had that were similar. It was so awesome--so like God to answer my specific prayer. I haven't seen her since that consequential meeting at the ice cream shack, yet I continue to pray for her.

WOMAN FROM A MUSLIM COUNTRY

One never knows what opportunities God will bring. One afternoon I had what I considered an amazing opportunity with a college student from Pakistan. She, along with several other students from a nearby college, were at the clubhouse in my housing complex giving of their time to their community by serving us ice cream sundaes and banana splits. After serving us ice cream each college student picked a table at which to sit and talk with the tenants. My table was the only table left with no college student sitting there, and the Pakistani student was the only college person left who needed a place to sit (was that God or was that God!?) I saw her scanning the room and caught her eye and motioned for her to come and sit with us ladies.

Even though this seems to be against what Christianity teaches, I sometimes do not bring up the subject of God or the Bible on my own. I often veer into the subject of Christianity subtly mentioning other subjects that could lead to the subjects of spirituality or God, and then wait for the person or persons to bring up the subject and then I have my 'in'. The student asked what I did to keep myself busy which led me to tell her about my Christian T.V. show which I produce myself; I kept it short; she was captivated. She began talking to me about her family life growing up in her country; about her religion which she did not believe in and many more things. Mostly, she was very interested in Christianity and flooded me with question after question. She wasn't content with short, generic answers; she wanted details--and details she got!

Firstly, I explained to her about the Body of Christ being 'an organism vs an organization'--that Jesus is the Head and we are the branches. I then explained 'receiving rather than just believing'--receiving Christ as our Lord and believing and receiving what He did for mankind.

The young woman was smitten. "I have never heard anything like this in my life", she told me. I told her if she ever needed family (as she had been in New England for a long time separated from her family,) to call me and I would have her over and make spaghetti for her.

If we do our part in sharing the gospel, God will do His part in bringing them into His kingdom.

THE PHONE STORE

Two days after I prayed for more opportunities to share Christ, I had to go to the phone store because I was losing half of my calls on my brand, new cell phone. I perched myself up on one of their high chairs as I explained my technical problem to the saleswoman. With my phone in hand she made her way to a back room to connect it with the company's computers in another state (or something like that.) Although she did not return for nearly a half hour, I was not bothered at all; in fact, it felt so good to get out of the house; I was enjoying the relaxation. Eventually the young woman returned to where I was seated. I was careful not to break her concentration as she thumbed with two cell phones, mine and one that belonged to the company, yet when there was a lull, when she was waiting for a call back, I opened my mouth to speak because I did not want to lose the opportunity to say something spiritual. I don't have a clue what I said, but I knew I connected with her spirit because she was quick to tell me that she had just started going back to church after years of being away from the Lord.

The showroom was void of people so she relaxingly posed many questions to me which I welcomed. I ended up telling her that I was a writer to which she asked if I wrote books. I told her that I did, that I wrote Christian testimonies; that put a smile on her face. Her demeanor led me to tell her a story that I knew she would enjoy hearing about my being in that store one evening a few years earlier when no one but myself and a young salesman were in the store. I pointed to a table and high stool across the room, and told her that it was where I sat with the young man when my cell phone rang. The caller happened to be my publisher and we actually conducted a business deal right there over the phone in the phone store. I was so excited that I told the salesman that when I received my first shipment of books I was going to give him the first copy; he got really excited. When the books were delivered I remembered what I had told the young man and autographed a book and took it to him at the phone store.

The saleswoman was blown away as I relayed the story. I also had a chance to tell her about some funny happenings regarding people I did not know texting me. How she laughed! So you see--it's not as difficult as we make it to be in our minds to talk to people about Jesus.

TONS OF OPPORTUNITIES

I have so many dear Christian friends on Facebook who light up my life every, single day. They pray with me, and I with them when there is a need. They share encouraging and inspiring stories with me. They fill my life with joy and happiness, and bless me to no end. Through these friendships I am provided with a multitude of opportunities to express my beliefs and convictions, to counsel, to instruct, to take counsel, to take instruction, to encourage others, to share the gospel, and so much more.

People from all over the world public and private message me on a continual basis with important prayer requests. Families I worked for in the early 1990's and early 2000's write and ask me to pray for their loved ones; those requests, especially, touch my heart.

Being able to comfort a friend or acquaintance that has lost someone is a blessed opportunity. Sending birthday blessings (sometimes five in one day) blesses others. In 2012 I received over 200 birthday messages from my friends. I spent the whole day answering each one, individually, but it was worth it because of the joy each one brought.

I cannot imagine what my senior years would be like had Facebook not evolved. Every time a friend posts a Bible verse I am built up. Every time a friend comments on one of my posts I am built up. Every time a friend posts a Christian song or video, I am built up. Every time they make me laugh, I am blessed.

Laughter is so necessary for the soul, and Facebook is the perfect avenue to post something funny. church messages, event information, the death of mutual friends, world news, the plights of martyrs, stories of physically challenged people-- we all share the same heartbeat. We need each other.

A SWEET TIME

"Want to go for lunch with me?" I asked a church member one Sunday after the service was over. "Sure". Donna followed me in her car to a nearby Mexican restaurant. After peering at the distinct species of fish in the fish tanks, we were led by a hostess to a booth. Each of us had difficulty choosing an entrée as there were several appetizing choices on the menu. I decided on a taco salad while Donna went with enchiladas.

Underneath the gaiety and small talk I was praying silently as one of my objectives was to minister to my acquaintance's hurting heart. Instinctively, I discerned that she would not be overly forthcoming about her life or her heartbreak; I would never veer any farther than where she would take me. It would be fulfilling to witness God touch someone that I was ministering to; yet, it doesn't always go that way. Sometimes all one can do is to say a few words and to trust God to magnify them afterward, which is the way the conversation seemed to be going.

When we fill ourselves with the Holy Spirit renouncing any and every small part of ourselves, God can take over a conversation so remarkably even as to astound us. And that is precisely what He did that afternoon. The woman with whom I was dining began to shed tears as she confessed to me that my conversation had helped her immensely giving her renewed hope. I was dumbfounded as I intentionally held back somewhat for fear that I might intimidate her. We never know.

All that we need to do is to look to see who God wants us to spend time with, you know, like a sea captain scanning the ocean wide with binoculars scouting the massive waters to see which way to embark. The opportunities are all around us.

VARIOUS OPPORTUNITIES

Some opportunities are not meant to be life changing for others; yet, they allow us to show forth goodness and righteousness. The following stories attest to this:

One afternoon the Holy Spirit stopped me from writing and had me contact my friend Sam to see how he was doing as it had been a quite a few months since we last spoke. Knowing that he was working part time I sent him a text rather than to call him. 'Call when you are able to talk,' I wrote. He replied, 'I'm on my way to an appointment…will call later.' He called a few hours later.

Sam and I caught up on different things and toward the end of our conversation he told me how that a young woman who was visiting someone in the run -down apartment building in which he lived was out in the hallway crying one day. He felt sorry for her and had her to go into his room to comfort her. While she was in his room he had to use the bathroom which was located down at the end of a long hallway. When he walked back to his room she was gone along with some of his jewelry handed down to him from his deceased grandfather, his D.V.D.'s, collectible coins and other miscellaneous items.

I felt so bad for him because he had next to nothing as it was, and no money to replace anything. "Sam, I bought a bunch of D.V.D.'s at a tent sale this past summer and haven't gotten around to watching them and probably never will. I am going to mail them to you. I will discard the casings and place them in lightweight sleeves and put them in mailers and mail them to you. I'm going to package them up right now before I forget. Consider them a Christmas present".

"Thank you B.J. God is so faithful. He always replaces what we lose, but I don't have anything to give you for Christmas". "You don't have to give me anything, Sam, just call me up and wish me a Merry Christmas". "Thank you, B.J.".

Not only did the Lord use me to lighten Sam's load that day, He enlarged my heart by giving me the opportunity to do something good for another human being. Read on…

I was traveling south on the Maine Turnpike and stopped at the rest stop in Kennebunk to use the facilities. I was the only woman in the ladies room. After I exited the stall I washed my hands at the sink where I discovered a ring near the faucet. I could tell that the gem was of value. I picked it up and as I walked out into the crowded restaurant area, I asked God to show me somebody who looked as if they were in a panic. My eyes gazed from one white, round table to another, from one fast food stand to another, from one end of the building to the other looking for the person who apparently used the restroom, and took off her beautiful ring while washing her hands and forgot to put it back on her finger when she was finished.

Five minutes later I saw a young, blonde girl wearing a uniform similar to other workers at the rest area. She was running directly for the women's rest room. I was positioned near the exit to the parking lot thinking that someone would come running in from the outside. I hurriedly walked toward the ladies room and caught up with the young woman as she walked out with a look of dire disappointment on her face. "Are you looking for something", I asked. "Yes, I left my ring on the sink in there", I smiled and handed her the ring. "I found it and have been searching for you. I asked God to show me someone who looked stressed as if she had lost something. As soon as I saw you running and noticed how scared you looked, I realized it had to be you. I could tell that your ring is a birthstone. Please be very careful with it in the future". Read on…

In November 2013 I was shopping in a Dollar Store in Sanford, Maine when I found a credit card and folded money on the floor in the back of the store; no one was around. I put the card and money in my pocket and

pg. 132

began looking for the person who dropped them probably from her pocket. I prayed the same prayer that I prayed when I found the girl's ring, "Lord, please show me someone who looks panicky". No one fit the description so I headed to the check out register where I planned to report finding the card and money. As I was headed in that direction I spotted a woman walking briskly into the store and appearing somewhat stressed heading toward the back wall. I suspected that it was the woman who lost her possessions. I turned my cart around and started walking toward her. I tried to catch up to her, but she was out of sight by the time I got turned around. I practically ran with the cart, yet could not find her, so I hurried to the register figuring she would be there reporting her loss; she was.

I heard her say to the check out person, "It has to be here someplace". "Did you lose a credit card?" I asked. The woman's face lit up. "Yes". "I have your card and money". I explained everything to her as I handed her the items. I even explained to her and the check out person how that I prayed and asked God to help me find her.

I am not ashamed to publicly give God the credit for things that happen. Few words were exchanged between the woman and I, mainly thank you and you're welcome; yet, I made her day. I am certain that she will never forget the horrible feeling that accompanied her not knowing if she would ever find the card. In fact, the night before I had watched a movie about identity theft in America, and how that people's lives have been turned upside down from losing their credit cards. That made my finding that credit card even more wonderful. It pleases God so much when we are ready to do what is right and good. That is precisely why He inspired the Apostle Paul to write in the Book of Ephesians to put on the breastplate of righteousness when we put on the armor of God.

CHAPTER 11

INTIMACY

HE FULFILLS ALL MY DESIRES

I don't need viewers to write to me via the T.V. stations on which my shows are aired or to call to give me encouragement; God is doing it…

Psalm **68**:11… '…the women who bear and publish (the news) are a great host'…

In Song of Solomon 2:4 God asks to hear my voice; I call that intimate.

Do I have a constant sense of my Shepherd's presence, regardless of my surroundings? Do I take time to meet my Good Shepherd each day letting Him tell me of His love, and cheering His heart with my interest in Him? Do I realize that my voice lifted in praise and song is sweet to Him, or do I withhold it? When He asks to hear my voice, what do I tell Him?

After doing T.V for going on four years, I have not had one note from viewers giving me kudos for the work I am doing. But it is O.K. because God gives me kudos all the time regarding my show. Many friends along the Maine coast regularly watch the show. The son of some friends even regularly watches it. Family members of my neighbors watch the show. Diversified church people and friends watch it on you tube and a certain few are unbelievably faithful and complimentary that they make up for dozens. I would rather have their few heartfelt comments then a whole drawer full of notes.

THE SONGS KEEP COMING

As I lay in bed one morning with my eyes closed, I heard these words to a song from the 50's playing in my mind, "…giving up my throne to marry you". It was a fun song sung by Doris Day and it had to do with her becoming a princess. In the song she tells of giving up her throne to marry her lover--an amazing sacrifice of love. Well, it immediately dawned on me that Jesus gave up His throne to marry us. He came to earth to live with us and He will come back to get His bride; this is what the Spirit of God interpreted the song to mean. How very precious!

SO ROMANTIC

Another song sung to me by my heavenly Lover as I awoke from sleep:

I think it is the chorus…

"You, you, you---I'm in love with you, you, you….

Take me in your arms please do---say you love me too, too, too….

We were meant for each other---as sure as the heavens above….

We were meant for each other---to have to hold and to love…

HERE'S ANOTHER

Be my, be my baby---translation: be My, be My baby---God singing to me....

AND ANOTHER

Heavenly Lover, heavenly Lover---all of your kisses are telling me this is the way it should be....(I must have been singing this one to Him in my sleep.)

AND ANOTHER

Graduation's almost here my love---teach me tonight...(referring to the rapture and our going to heaven)...

Dancing with my heavenly Lover.....being kissed....Him gazing at me...

AND, OF COURSE, I CAN'T WRITE ABOUT SOME THINGS...

MARITAL BLISS

I was at my granddaughter's wedding reception in September 2013 when the bridal couple embraced and sporadically kissed during the afternoon. I loved watching them. I got to thinking: You know how at wedding receptions the guests tap their cups and glasses with spoons to produce a resounding noise to get the bridal couple to kiss? Well...this couple didn't give us a chance to do that one time. I could only assimilate their affection for one another with Jesus' affection for us. He is always kissing us with the kisses of His mouth. He doesn't give us a chance to tap a cup or glass with a spoon to make the familiar resounding noise (so to speak)...He is the Initiator. Daily, I feel like a bride....oh wait....I am a bride....part of the bride of Christ.....such joy...such unspeakable joy!!!!!

NO ENCUMBRANCES

One wintry day it was frigid here the Northeast. I had put anti-freeze in my gas tank at the beginning of the week, but each day it got colder and colder. I began to wonder if I should put more anti-freeze in the gas tank, but it was too cold for me to go out to start my car. The following day I put on layers of outerwear including three hats and two scarves, and went outside to start my car which started on the first turn....yea! I wanted the engine to run for a while so I sat there trying not to concentrate on the cold.

I wasn't very far from my front door; yet, I may as well have been 1,000 miles away because I was distanced from all the things that cluttered my mind--everything on my 'to do' list. What came to my mind was the $60.00 that my house guest left in my daily devotional on my bedside table over the weekend. I was shocked to receive the gift, yet I wanted to accept it graciously and not give her a hard time.

As the engine revved up, my mind continued to ponder about the sizable gift. One third of that amount would have been too much so far as I was concerned. And then it came to me: Two weeks prior to that day, I traveled to New Hampshire to visit a good friend of mine who is like a son to me; who was released from prison after serving a term of over 20 years during which time I was his only visitor. We couldn't wait to have lunch together on the outside. What a delightful reunion it turned out to be.

As I drove home on the Maine Turnpike I thought about when and if I would ever be able to afford to meet with him again in the future. I began to calculate the cost of gas for the trip, the cost for the tolls and the money I spent for our lunch. It added up to $60.00. I couldn't afford it, but I was happy to obey the Lord and to make the trip to bless a man who spent most of his twenties, all of his thirties and more than half of his forties incarcerated. And then I got the connection---the reason that God had my house guest leave me $60.00 is because that is the exact amount of money I spent to bless someone two weeks prior.

I also realized that God waited until I had those uninterrupted, few moments to reveal that thought to me. Praise Him.

AN ICE CREAM CAKE

On Easter Saturday 2013 I planned to treat myself to an ice cream at a local creamery. I had been there just one time to check it out and to buy some ice cream cupcakes. While there the salesperson let me have a sample of their mint ice cream that they made right on the premises. I wanted to go back for some ice cream cake made with the same mint ice cream. I headed there, but to my disappointment they were closed down. It didn't surprise me because their prices were quite high; I did not know how they could stay in business. I scouted the area to see where I could buy some ice cream cake to satisfy my insatiable craving; I couldn't find anyplace nor did I want to resort to the freezer section of a supermarket.

The next day, Easter Sunday, my pastor and his wife put on a big Easter dinner after church. What a feast! We had ham, potatoes, corn, carrots, vinegar cabbage, salad and rolls. I was stuffed to the gills when I saw my pastor's mother get up and go into the kitchen. The next thing I knew she was cutting large slices of what appeared to be a dessert to pass out. Could that be what I thought it was? Could that be an ice cream cake? Sure enough. God knew how disappointed I was the preceding day when I was unable to have the ice cream cake that I craved, and He satisfied my craving by the kindness of my pastor's mother and father who took it upon themselves to buy the cake for all of us to enjoy.

THE MARSHMALLOW EGG

On Easter Sunday 2013 a member of my congregation, Albert, passed out chocolate, marshmallow Easter eggs to everyone who came to church that morning. Because I live alone and haven't colored Easter eggs or made up baskets in so many years, the candy egg with the bunny wrapper on it touched my heart more than a rare gem would have. It was as if Jesus, Himself, gave me something special. It showed me that the small things in life are the biggest. I don't think I will ever forget it.

INDIA'S BOAST

One time Oprah had the most beautiful woman in the world that was from India as a guest on her show. The woman's face was perfectly symmetrical with tantalizing eyes and glamorous features; she was mesmerizing. Her beautiful, Indian attire and beads enhanced her beauty. Years later the woman's image came up on my Facebook page. Again, I was spellbound that anyone could be so beautiful.

I wished that I could be that pretty. The Holy Spirit hastily answered my thoughts by revealing to me that God is even more mesmerized with Spirit-filled Christians than the world is with good looking people because Jesus dwells on our hearts, and God only sees Jesus when He looks at us. The brilliance of His Son produces a resplendent effect to the Father.

ALONE (although not completely alone)

I am alone the biggest part of the time. I spend most of my time writing. Writing used to be enjoyable, but because of my debilitating back condition I can no longer sit at my desk and use the keyboard without experiencing a lot of pain. I rigged up a way to type by placing my hard drive on a file cabinet near the end of my bed and placing my monitor on my antique dressing table next to my bed which isn't even near the wall but touching my bed. I position myself against a big stack of pillows with my legs outstretched with the keyboard on my lap. This may seem like an ideal position in which to write; yet, it is not. Hardly anything is at arm's reach. I have to get up and down to go from my bed to my desk

pg. 139

several times a day for writing supplies which is good insofar as getting exercise; yet, having things within arm's reach would allow me to do my job much more easily and without interrupting the flow of writing. I do keep reference books nearby, however.

When one is called to write for the Lord, he/she must record God's notes all through the days no matter where he/she is at. He/she must pour out what comes from God and not let thoughts become stagnant within, and then the Spirit of God fills us up again with new thoughts. The more we share with others, the more He fills us up again.

To reiterate, my bedroom/ office is where I spend most of my life. I watch the news on T.V. for 5 minutes at noon and at 5 in the evening. I incorporate housework into writing and not the other way around. At one point in time in the fall of 2013 I began to wonder if I was insane. It was not just a fleeting thought; it stayed with me for the better part of a week. And then, after a Sunday night church service our small congregation was rapping about the message when my missionary friend Dennis spoke about a great woman of God, Amy Carmichael, who, while lying in bed for 20 years from sickness, ministered to scores of people. Then my friend Joyce spoke about Praying Hyde who lived in one room and spent most of his time in the room praying. Within seconds the Holy Spirit revealed to me that I was in no way insane; that His will for me was to remain in my room, alone with Him, writing and praying the biggest part of my time.

To say that my concern was lifted would be an understatement; I was blown away. It was more than edification; it was Godly intimacy.

UNA GRANDE BESO

It was a morning from hell. I was on the phone and computer all morning long with the computer geeks. Because I was having trouble with my cell phone, and because I wasn't getting good reception in my bedroom where my computer is located, I couldn't make out what the agents were saying, and had to have them repeat things over and over…what a fiasco…my mind was frazzled.

When things like that happen I am reminded of a message preached by a pastor friend of mine one time. He preached that there is no such thing as a bad day. That meant that I had to go to God and ask Him for His grace for me to calm down, and to wait patiently for the agent to update and fix any problems on my p.c. via remote. I employed that same technique when I dealt with the phone company which I had to deal with by way of the Internet and not by phone.

Soon after everything had been resolved and I felt like burying my head in my pillow and going to sleep, I checked out the newsfeed on you tube instead. The Holy Spirit said in His still small voice to look to see if an old friend had joined Facebook; sure enough he had. I immediately connected with the son of my dear girlfriend from Cuba, Leandro, who now lives in Spain. He private messaged me a cartoon with these words written on it: una grande beso….one big kiss. It was as if Jesus, Himself, was kissing me.

The cartoon not only blessed me; it cleared my fuzzy head.

CHAPTER 12

TRIALS

THEY KEEP ME ON MY KNEES

Everyone, I don't care who it is, has trials in their lives; there are no exceptions (if they don't seem to have, trust me--they will have sooner or later.) Whether the trials pertain to our physical bodies; to our involvement in accidents; finances, broken hearts or fears, God allows them to teach us to rely on Him for help. The Bible teaches us that trials are not about us, that they are about Him. My youngest son is a rock climber; he defies fear. He does not discuss his adventures with me; yet, I view the photos of rock climbers that he posts on Facebook and these photos put my heart in my mouth. One may not think of this as a trial; yet, the sport he has chosen robs me of peace of mind, and so in that regard, it is a trial for me. Of course, I hand it over to God. I just wish I didn't keep taking it back.

This same son is also a deep sea fisherman. Just about every excursion a fisherman takes out to sea becomes an odyssey. He refuses to tell me about the worst of the death defying escapades he has been in as not to frighten me; however, the ones I do know about are scary enough. I am a glutton for punishment and I watch videos of dangerous deep sea adventures on you tube; consequently, my son's safety is always on my mind; I am getting better though.

My second son owns a communications company. He has been climbing 1,000 to 2,000 foot towers for numerous years. My grandson climbs the towers also. This is one of the most high risk jobs in the country with repeated casualties. It makes me crazy to think about it so I give it all to God.

My third son digs clams for a living in the summer. Continuous bending makes for an 80 year-old back on a young man. His hands have become like ground beef plus he suffers from carpel tunnel syndrome. My mother's heart aches because of these factors. Even more worrisome than those issues are the fights that diggers have at the clam flats because of government regulations and more. One of the diggers actually showed up at the flats with a loaded gun one day and threatened to shoot my son. That is why I cover my kids with Christ's Blood every, single day.

My oldest son gives me cause to worry, as well. I have heard reports from his wife that he scares the neighbors half to death when he stands on his slanted roof acting fearless when working on their house and when putting up lights for Christmas.

REACTION

I had a severe reaction to a new prescription drug and ran into double trouble because I had taken another prescription drug a half hour earlier. My heart rate was approx 600 beats per minute---I counted 100 beats in 10 seconds and multiplied it by 6. My whole body shook uncontrollably. I kept drinking fluids. I was so dizzy, weak and nauseated that I could barely stand up. I refused to let my family take me to the E.R. It was more important for me to get on Facebook and to have my church Body pray for me than to be taken to the hospital. Responses poured in right away, and as soon as they did my heart rate went back to normal in a fraction of a second---it was amazing! What power! That was the power that the Apostle Paul displayed when he called demons out of a woman in the Book of Acts 16: 14-18 where they came out instantly and the woman was healed.

I was on the phone with the doctor a number of times during the day. I forced myself to vomit by eating some lousy tasting, spicy soup that I brought home from a restaurant the night before. Within a short while I felt somewhat better. I vomited twice more. I just had to ride it out. That night I could hardly sleep from being so wound up. The episode lasted for over 20 hours.

I blamed myself as I always tell the doctors to give me half doses of prescription meds because of my small size, and I forgot to remind them of it that time. To add to the existing dilemma, I crushed the pill and took it with pudding without checking with the pharmacy. I blamed myself for what happened because I forgot to take just a half of a dose of the new pill. God came through, nevertheless; He always does.

SLEEP PARALYSIS

For a number of years I have had infrequent episodes in the middle of the night whereby I lose my breath and become paralyzed not being able to move even a muscle. It is the most frightening experience anyone could possibly imagine. During these episodes just before I lose consciousness, I beg Jesus, in my thoughts to help me as I have no use of my mouth. I struggle vehemently to call out to Him, "Jesus, help me, Jesus, help me, Jesus, help me". If He did not answer me when calling His name I would die—beyond question.

During one such horrible episode when I couldn't move or breathe for a protracted period of time, I kept saying to myself that the only way to get through it was to tell myself that I was going through the suffering so that my kids wouldn't have to go through it. Conclusively, in desperation, I forced myself with everything I had in me to take a deep breath through my mouth and to use my inhaler in the nightmare. Immediately, the inhaler took effect and I started to breathe in small breaths. The Holy Spirit, knowing what I had been through, blessed me and gave me renewed hope by singing to me a song from the 50's, 'Teach Me Tonight'. There is a line in the lyrics that goes: 'Graduation's almost here, my love'. That would refer to our graduation into heaven as

Christians. What more meaningful words could He have given me as I came out of that hellish trial?

I went for two sleep apnea studies, one of which showed inconclusive results, and another of which showed that I do not have sleep apnea pur se'; yet, I do have an even worse condition called sleep paralysis which is positively horrible.

For 15 years or so I have occasionally cried out, 'mommy, mommy" in my sleep. I always become terrified when calling out for her. I believe that this happens because of something that has been in my subconscious mind for my whole life. It is just a mystery why it never revealed itself until I was in my 50's. At the age of four I witnessed my brother being burned in a fire which caused him to have his leg amputated, and which left his remaining leg and his torso horribly scarred. My parents were at my uncle's wedding at the time and a teenage aunt babysat for us three kids. I must have screamed my little heart out, and not having my mother near-by, I must have buried my fear and trauma in my subconscious mind.

Like everyone else Christians go through trials. The thing of it is that with Christ in our lives we have an 'in' to His resources and help; we have an 'in' to the throne of God with our prayers. Because I have prayed and asked my church members to pray with me, these episodes have decreased tremendously; they will continue to decrease. One of the reasons I believe they are decreasing is because God has shown me that if I sleep on a stack of pillows (4 or 5) rather than lying flat in bed, that I do not seem to be afflicted as much. Another trick I discovered which was confirmed by the doctor and nurses is that after I switched my sleeping position and started to sleep at the other end of my bed not being able to see the large room around me, my middle of the night problems decreased considerably; there is safety in a small, safe place. God answers in a variety of ways, yet He does answer.

OVERTIME

The devil and his demons are always working overtime in getting us to get caught up in the pressures of life. We have so many more things today to make life easier and to take the stress off our minds---things like online banking, computers, ipads, cell phones and all the rest. We are happy to acquire the products; yet, we forget about the technical garbage that we have to put up with in dealing with problems that pertain to our gadgets. I, as well as everyone else, have to deal with these problems and many times have come close to taking an ax to my computer. I have spent countless hours dealing with the bank over online banking problems with my online account when it was seemingly compromised. I have also spent countless hours dealing with the phone company, electric company and my Internet service provider dealing with computer problems, and that is not to mention having to take my hard drive in to the geeks for service four times a year. When I am plagued with these things, which is much too often, I am at God's mercy. I absolutely have to give all these situations to Him.

A WATCHMAN

The Christian community is no exception when it comes to having people with the same common denominator as you coming against you even more so than the world coming against you when your thoughts are different than theirs. You may be taking orders from God Who is the Head One; yet, you can be damned if you do and damned if you don't even amongst the brethren. But, if you have a calling on your life, it is to be expected. It is easy to fall into the mindset of, 'don't I give it all already?' 'For what do I need this aggravation?' We must put on the armor of God each day to ward off this thinking from taking over our minds.

SANDY HOOK

A week before Christmas in 2012 the life of every American was affected when the Sandy Hook School massacre occurred. Sandy Hook is a small town in Connecticut which is a section of the lucrative Newtown. My family lived in Sandy Hook in the 1960's. There was a joke going around at that time which described Sandy Hook as the ghetto of Newtown. Many of the one -family dwellings, like ours, were modest ranch houses, yet there were some really beautiful, big homes there too. Ours was a three-bedroom ranch on a corner acre of land in a community of young families. Our kids were in scouts and played sports. I was a teacher aide in the kindergarten class at Sandy Hook School.

Whoever would think that a small place like that could make national headlines drawing to its high school the President of the United States to address grieving families. But it did.

Twenty -six people including 20 first graders were shot at close range, some kids being shot 11 or more times by a 20 year- old gunman who killed his mother at their home before heading to the school to carry out the rest of his malicious plan before killing himself. His mother had been a teacher aide at the school according to reports.

When all the T.V. stations carried the news everyone in the nation was glued to our T.V. screens. The killings were especially close to home for me and my family. It was as if time had stood still and we were again residents of that small community. My sons were able to picture the inside of the school building and the surroundings. We couldn't even speak to or look at one another without tears coming to our eyes, or without our hearts being ripped open. The event will always be with us.

My heart is heavy more than it is light some weeks. At my age someone I know dies almost on a semi-weekly basis. Because I have so many friends and acquaintances, news of a death comes to my computer just about every day. It is virtually impossible to have a light heart when death comes at this speed. I don't care how close to God a person may be; when one receives bad news on an ongoing basis it affects a person's soul. It takes prayer and God to raise a person above all the bad news.

NOISE

To live in a single family home and then to have to move to a senior apartment comprised of 650 square feet of space is not only an unpleasant step down; having to endure noises from adjacent apartments consisting of blasting T.V.'s because of neighbors who are hard of hearing, cabinet doors being slammed all day long, toilet seats slamming against toilets, noises from pets, noises from tenants snoring loudly and walking around during the night when you are trying to sleep and a host more of additional disturbances make life anything but bearable.

I have always been a reader; yet, the pleasure of reading had been taken from me for a couple of years because I could not concentrate on reading because of the noise from the other side of my apartment wall. I couldn't read out on my patio because of loud T.V.'s or loud talking coming from other yards on my street. During short seasons in the spring and fall I was able to sit in my car and read with the windows rolled down, and I was deliriously happy for those times; yet, they were not my preference.

At the time I had done everything from sleep on an air mattress in my living room for eight months at a time to barricade myself in my bedroom for several months at a time which produced a feeling of suffocation. Was God trying to teach me to endure all situations and to stop complaining? I know one thing…He used it. In what way, you may wonder? When I moved from that place, my next apartment, although just another senior apartment, has been like a mansion to me. I love it much more than I ordinarily would have loved it because of what I went through in my former apartments.

The bottom line has always been that I want to stay unmoved in spirit as a disciple and never to be displeasing to God in any way.

45 DEGREES

Growing older has its minuses; that is for sure. My spinal condition started when I was a young girl so I can't blame it on age; yet, age has contributed to it greatly since deterioration of my vertebrae has progressed increasingly as I have gotten older. Can you imagine what it is like to be told that your spine is at a 45 degree angle shaped like the letter V? Can you imagine the tip of the letter V sticking out of my back? That is the news I was given. I should wonder what the future holds for me or how much of a future that I will have, but all I hold onto is a heart vision I had one time of what I would look like in heaven.

I think it is a gift of God that I am not consumed with negativity concerning the condition of my spine. Thousands of men, women and children around the world are a lot worse off than I.

CHAPTER 13

LAUGHTER

GOD'S SPOUSE

My grandson Dave and his twins David and Makayla surprised me with a visit on Mother's Day in 2012. It was their first time in my new apartment and David Jr. was intrigued with a puzzle I had on my wall of the risen Jesus with Mary Magdalene at His feet. David's grandmother, Brenda, my daughter-in law, asked him, "Do you know who that is?"

"Yes, that's God and His wife".

GAVIN

My son, Tony, called one day and I immediately sensed excitement in his voice. He said that a family friend, Gavin, called him and said, "Tony, you're not going to believe this. I saw your mother on T.V. I videoed the show for you". Tony was so proud of me that he busted with joy. He conveyed to me his reply to Gavin, "Now that you've seen her, listen to what she has to say". I couldn't wait to e-mail my friend Rachael about it to build her up because she got to meet Gavin one time.

NANA'S ON T.V.

My future grandson-in -law happened to catch my show at my son's house early one morning and ran through the house hollering to my granddaughter, "Nana's on T.V… Nana's on T.V.!!!!!!!" They could not wait to tell me.

FOR WOMEN ONLY:

STOPPED BY A POLICEMAN

After a long day's drive up the Maine coast to visit friends in 90 degree heat, and after getting together with church members for fellowship and for an evening church service, I was pretty warn out. I was short-winded to boot since my asthmatic condition was aggravated by my wearing a bra for so many hours causing tightness around my chest. Oh the joys of womanhood…

The church service that we held in a community room at a retired pastor friend's complex wasn't quite over; yet, I left early to head down the coast before it got any darker. Immediately after getting into my car I unsnapped my bra, but did not slip it off because of some people hanging out in the parking lot. I waved a final goodbye as I drove off. After leaving Rockland I drove through the small town of Thomaston where the speed limit is only 25 miles per hour. I used to live in the adjacent town and traveled that road a thousand times having been quite familiar with the speed limit and obeying it. I don't know what came over me that night, but I wasn't thinking about how fast I was going; all that I could think about was taking off my bra. I slipped the left strap off my arm and then the right strap. As I did so I realized I had both straps pinned to my summer top so that they would not show, therefore my bra was still half on and half off; I couldn't take it completely off. I also realized that I am a person who cannot walk and chew gum at the same time. As soon as that important realization wiggled into my frontal lobes, it came to me that as I attempted to free myself of the cumbersome clothing, my foot pressed down harder on the accelerator. "What am I doing?" I asked myself as I discovered what I had done. I slowed down...but...it was too late; lights on a police car were blinking and a policeman was right on my tail.

I pulled over and looked down at my bra sticking out of my blouse on either side. I sat there like a first class idiot. What went through my mind was that the stupid devil was reacting to the marvelous time I had with my church friends. A subsequent thought went through my mind, as well: I thought of the fine I might get and that I didn't have any money to pay it.

The policeman walked toward my car. I could see him coming in my rearview mirror. He wasn't happy; his frown and demeanor announced that to me. "Hello. What did I do wrong?" "You were going 37 miles an hour in a 25 mile an hour zone". He continued to scold me as if I were a little child. "I am *sooooo* embarrassed, officer. I have been in this awful heat all day and night, and I have asthma and my bra felt tight and I was having a problem breathing so I tried taking it off while driving. I only managed to get it half way off when I realized that I was speeding".

 I was mortified!

The officer reached out to take hold of my documents and sauntered back to the police car momentarily and then came back. "You know, the fine for speeding is $189.00". I looked at him dead -on and said sheepishly, "I don't have it; I'm on social security". "I know you don't", he replied. "I know you're not interested in hearing this I said to him, but this is only the second time I have been stopped by a policeman in all the years I have been driving. I used to live up here and I have always respected the 25 mile an hour rule". "Listen", he said sternly, "I'm going to let you go, but the next time you're driving and you want to take off your bra, pull over to the side of the road". "I will, officer, this will never happen again. Thank you so much. God bless you and God bless your family". "Thank you", he said.

I guarantee that the policemen in his station talked about the woman who tried to unsnap and remove her bra while driving for a long time afterward.

I am still thanking God for His mercy.

DEAR ABBY

I wasn't sure where to place this comical vignette--in the chapter with my schedule or elsewhere, so I am placing it here in the laughter chapter. I make myself laugh when I think of the number of people I keep in touch with via Facebook as busy as I am with writing and so many other things. Let me give you a 'for instance'. Not only do I counsel extensively on the net--guys as well as gals-- my chat window pops up with a 'what's up' from a girlfriend's grandson's friend who befriended me, and whom I do not have the heart to ignore, every time he is home from school. The kid is no more than nine years-old. So funny.

I also get majorly sentimental toward the guys with whom my granddaughters have broken up. They have become such losses to our family. I still get caught up in their problems and I take their problems on myself. I am a glutton for punishment.

I could write a book about the messages I get from guys from all parts of the world-messages that would crack you up. One guy told me all about his qualities and what a catch he was in detailed description. He was totally into what an awesome guy he was-- thanks, but no thanks. Another guy emphasized that he was into older women and even married an older woman who eventually passed away. He went on to tell me all the things she did for him taking care of him like she was his mother. He soaked up her attention. Oh my! I ended up changing the settings on my account.

THE PAN

My brother -in-law insisted that I get rid of some of my pans when he and my sister visited in the summer of 2012. In fact, he gave me a boost in cleaning out my cupboards by showing me what to get rid of and by going out and buying me a really nice frying pan with a glass lid. He called to my attention that when Teflon peels off pans it can be dangerous as some bits of it can go into food we are cooking.

After my family went back home I began to throw out more of my old pans; one was a favorite. Afterward, I realized that I could have used the pan for outdoor gardening work or any sort of thing other than cooking. Darn! A week later my youngest son had come by after returning to Maine from a trip. He was going through his duffle bag and came into the kitchen with a shiny pan the same size as the one I threw out, "Here mom---here's a pan for you".

I stood there with my mouth open.

BEDSIDE MANNER

As I was lying on the table waiting for my dreaded cortisone injection, my doctor asked his nurse out for dinner. I lay there wondering how bad the pain was going to be, and they are making plans about which restaurant to patronize etc. etc. I thought, 'Lord, you really have a sense of humor.' I really believe that he asked her out right when he was getting ready to jab me because he wanted me to relax (ultimately, You wanted me to relax)...YOU, precious One, are my Doctor...I love Your bedside manner.

APRIL FOOL'S JOKE

On April Fool's Day 2013 I texted my granddaughter telling her that I won the lottery for $1,000,000.00. I never in a million years dreamed that she would fall for it…but…bite the bait- hook, line and sinker- she did. She called me within minutes".You did what!" Because she never calls me, only texts me, I figured that I should tell her it was a gag. "It's April Fool's Day", I said. It turned out that everything had gone wrong for her that day, and she failed to see the humor in what I did; yet, unintentionally I received an actual phone call from her which was a first so I would say the joke went in my favor.

LEAVE IT TO AALIYAH

My granddaughter Rachael drove to my new apartment to visit me bringing along my great-granddaughter, Aaliyah, and one of her adult friends. It was a clear, pleasant day and after visiting in the house for a while, we all shifted outside to enjoy the sun. As we talked Aaliyah frolicked around the lawn entertaining herself and being inquisitive. The next thing we knew a little face with mischief in its eyes called out, "Look what I've got", holding up my spare house key that she had found hidden underneath one of my frog lawn ornaments. We tried to get it from her, but she ran from us as fast as her little tushie would take her.

That meant that I would have to find another hiding place for my spare key.

WHAT IN THE WORLD

Two months or so after I moved into my latest apartment, I finally figured out what the reason was behind pieces of my hair stuck to every envelope of my outgoing mail. The reason was that I organized my new desk differently from my old one. I kept a roll of scotch tape in a small wicker basket with handle along with my hairbrush and a few other items on my new desk in my new apartment. Apparently the hair from the hairbrush would attach to the scotch tape on the roll, and every time I went to tape an envelope a strand of hair would get stuck on the envelope under the tape. I'm glad that mystery was finally solved.

STOP THE CAR

When I visited my sister and brother-in-law in Connecticut in 2013, she cracked me up when she backed her car out of her garage as she usually did, only she must have been on automatic pilot because she had forgotten that my car was parked in one of the two spaces in her driveway. Thank God that my brother-in-law was standing right beside the driveway because she was not over far enough when she stepped on the throttle and backed up. Nick hollered, "Stop the car" just a second before she rammed into my car. Had she hit me it would have spoiled my vacation; yet, I could not help but laugh because we are all such creatures of habit.

CHAPTER 14

PERSONAL EDIFICATION

"…for your work shall be rewarded"… 2 Chronicles 15:7

"Old men shall dream dreams" … Joel 2:28

"He will guard the feet of the Godly ones"…Isaiah 2:9

AN INTERESTING E-MAIL

Some may wonder why I am including the following story in this book. The reason is that it reveals how God edifies His people. I received this e-mail from a dear friend in reference to a relative of hers with whom she wanted to fix me up a few years prior. As she relayed it she was surprised that this popped into her head the night before, and figured that I may have needed her to tell me (she was right; I did need her to tell me).

The e-mail read: 'You probably remember a few years ago when I told you about my cousin who lives in Maine, and how I wanted to have him meet you. That never worked out, but I thought I would take another stab at it, but then backed off. Anyway, I was relating this to Pastor (so and so) while my husband and I were visiting in his state and he asked, concerning my cousin, "Is he worthy of her?" He went on to say that he had done a Bible study at your house, and spoke very highly of you and your character etc. I thought that was very sweet of him and that you might want to know that.

Hope this blesses you,

Love, S.

Well, it did bless me; it blessed me, indeed. It caused me to feel worthiness about myself that I had never before felt. My friend's communication to me is an example of paying attention to our thoughts and not brushing them off thinking that they are crazy; they could very well be from God.

FLYING LIKE A BIRD

My pastor spoke about flying like a bird one Sunday morning. He spoke about flying away from the calamity that surrounds us. That part of His message was a confirmation of what God had given me during the week about flying like a bird. Being a senior I have not reached any spiritual plateau; however, I believe that God was telling me that I have reached a place where I can actually experience flying like a bird in the way I live my life.

We can learn a lot by studying birds. Birds are a big part of God's creation. He mentioned them in Genesis Chapter One. He also mentioned them in numerous places throughout the Bible. I love the way He speaks of the eagle in the Book of Isaiah. I love the thoughts of soaring like an eagle in my spiritual life with no encumbrances; this is what His desire is for each of us.

I got to thinking about birds and about the U.S. Air Force Thunderbirds who were scheduled to perform in my town for three days flying directly over my house. I began to think about myself soaring through the sky like one of the Thunderbirds flying in perfect formation with four other planes. My desire is to soar in my spiritual life and to stay in formation with the Trinity making every move in exact precision with the Three in One.

It is so easy to stray. Picture the Thunderbirds or the Navy's Blue Angels flying in perfect formation in the sky. One may leave the other planes taking a quick detour; yet, that plane glides gracefully right back into formation with the others. It is the same with us in Christ's Body. We may take a slight detour from the straight and narrow; yet, when we come back to where we belong by grace, He places us right back into the proper formation with the Godhead.

ROMEO

At a Bible study I attended one time, the person leading the study was talking about missionaries and those who have followed God not counting the cost. He asked, "Have you ever heard of anybody moving a great number of times to follow Christ?" I told him that I could relate to that---I was going into my 39th time---a gypsy for Jesus. Aside from the humor, though, I may not consider it sacrificial in that I just keep going along with Him as a part of life. God, on the other hand, showed me through the comment that Romeo made that God has much more than a ho-hum attitude toward my obedience in following Him through all the times I have moved.

A few months after I moved and returned to the place where Romeo conducted his Bible study, the same hall where I attended a Saturday night concert, it was wonderful to see him and the others again, and even more wonderful to take in the words that he spoke to me, "I will pray for you always" …heart to heart.

A BARRAGE

One of the ways that God has chosen to bless me in my work for Him is through hearing from dear family and friends on a daily basis. Using the keyboard in writing for T.V. and writing books for eight to 10 hours a day, and spending so much time by myself would get a little monotonous if I did not take hourly breaks to correspond with my friends on Facebook. Even before the social network evolved I corresponded with many friends via snail mail all through the years. The correspondence has kept me in the loop and enriched my life.

I am eternally grateful for the visits, phone calls, gifts, the abundant cards and letters, the e-mails, the messages, comments, posts, chats and the huge amount of support for my T.V. videos on You Tube. You, my beloved friends, keep me going.

UNIQUE EDIFICATION

God is unique to us all and speaks to us in our own language; not only in our own ethnic language but in our own, individual language--- our way of thinking, communication and understanding. For my morning devotional one morning the Holy Spirit led me to read from the Book of Isaiah that he (Isaiah) would affect the whole world. A few minutes later I turned on TBN Christian T.V. and an unfamiliar preacher was talking about Israel. He said that as small as Israel is (explaining how very small the country is,) it affects the whole world like no other country. A few minutes after that I listened to a weather person on T.V. and she began to explain la nina (the weather pattern) saying that it is sort of a sister to el nino. It had been unseasonably warm in the northeast, warm all through November and December--unbelievably warm. She proceeded to tell about how it started in the Pacific Ocean and had affected states as far away as Maine.

What all that said to me is that I am a very small person; yet, my ministry will reach out just like the Prophet Isaiah's, just like la nina and just like the tiny country of Israel and will affect many people and places. This is what I mean when I say that God speaks to us in our own language. It has nothing to do with self glorification; it has to do with believing Him by faith.

BUILT UP IN CHRIST

The best builder upper, of course, is the Word of God.

Take a look at Paul´s words in Acts 20:32. "And now, brethren, I commend you to God, and to the word of His grace, which is able to build you up, and to give you an inheritance among all them which are sanctified".

How are we 'built up? We are built up by the letter of the Word of God, in the power of the Spirit of grace, ministered in love. We are not to be concerned with knowledge, alone, for only the Spirit of God can convey the truth about knowledge.

Before we effectively minister to others, we must first learn to keep ourselves in the love of God. "Expect and patiently wait for the mercy of our Lord Jesus Christ" (Jude 21, Amplified).

Build yourself up in the most holy faith. Keep yourself in the love of God, and unconditional love will produce pure grace in transitional processes. Continue to pray in the Holy Spirit and look for God´s mercy - - always look for mercy! Build yourself up in the Word of Grace.

"As ye have therefore received Christ Jesus the Lord, so walk ye in him: Rooted and built up in him, and stablished in the faith, as ye have been taught, abounding therein with thanksgiving"…Colossians 2:6-7.

"But ye, beloved, building up yourselves on your most holy faith, praying in the Holy Spirit"…Jude 1:20.

These words are not only important, they are essential. If we are left alone with the enemy and his influences, we become prey to his accusations and criticism of ourselves. We need to cover our minds with the armor of God and to repeatedly build ourselves up in order to keep the enemy at a distance. Simply re-reading this entry reminds me of what I am in Christ's eyes, and of what I am not in Satan's eyes.

FEELING HELPLESS

I was sitting at my computer one Saturday afternoon caught up with everything in the house and with my projects. All I had to tackle was my following week's show. For the first time in three years of writing shows my mind went completely blank. From that awful place I went to a worse place; I felt as if my physical affliction had cornered me into helplessness. The pain, the physical limitations, my age, the whole nine yards…I was bombarded with negativity. How could I write or do anything constructive for God's kingdom? I asked myself…or I should say I told myself? But then, suddenly, I did an about face and stood my ground against the tempter. I searched for some notes on my computer and came up with the following, and as I began to read God inspired me from His Word:

The word 'steadfast' is derived from the word Hezomai which means to sit. Hedraios means to be sedentary or to stay seated. We are not to move from the seated position….we keep sitting. Paul meant these words figuratively, yet for me, personally, God, the Holy Spirit, meant them literally because I was doing a lot of sitting and lying down due to my back condition. He elaborated His message to me by communicating to me that I was being used no matter what my circumstances or physical limitations dictated; it was just like Him.

There I was in bed trying to alleviate some of the pressure from the base of my spine and God, in His unique-ness, ministered to me in my own language exactly what He knew would move me. He repetitiously used the words 'sitting and immovable'. No one in this world could have cared about where I was the way my heavenly Lover cared. He has always been and shall always be the ultimate Edifier.

SALLY'S COMMENT

One Christmas I gave away some C.D.'s of my songs to family and friends. A woman by the name of Sally who goes to my church called me on the phone to tell me that my C.D was the best Christmas present she received. She doesn't know it but she was the only recipient of my gift that remarked on it. Her comment was one of the most edifying comments I have ever received; it truly built me up.

JESUS' BAPTISM

Every Christian knows that Jesus did not have to be baptized...but...He was baptized; the reason being as it was explained to me was that Jesus had John, who felt that he was unworthy to baptize Jesus, to baptize Him in order to honor all that John had done for the kingdom of God; that speaks volumes. And, of course, He set an example for all of us. It shows us Jesus' character, His heart. What it spoke to me, personally, was that He sees everything I do for the kingdom and He appreciates it.

CHAPTER 15

FAITH

The Bible tells us to see what we wish for as it is already. When I pray with women who are having problems with family members; who are so broken that they can't get close to their family members; I encourage them to pray in the finished work. That means that if the prayer or wish is in alignment with the Holy Spirit that it is finished or done even before we ask for it, and that all we have to do is to exercise faith, to enter into rest and to wait for God's perfect timing for it to happen.

In the case of a family member who is not speaking to you, visualize that person's face minus a troubled countenance; visualize his/her face with a glad countenance. If the person's actions are appalling, picture that person with a calm expression, manifesting love and tenderness in your thoughts. There is no end to the ways we can visualize those who are unkind to us.

...the Word of God produces faith...

THE GIVER OF FAITH

From my notes…The spiritual is a few steps beyond where the natural would ever go…could ever go. How do we get there? Faith gets us there…faith motivated by love. The spiritual life is a response to grace by faith. Jesus Christ is the Giver of faith. All He had to do in bringing about healings when He was on earth was to speak a word. May we learn to exercise the faith of Jesus and nothing less that we may bring glory to the Father.

BE FAITHFUL IN THE LITTLE THINGS

I started out producing a T.V. show with one station which in a year's time went from one station to two stations all the way up to nine stations. From the inception I had a mindset not to go beyond 10 stations because I knew I would not be able to manage a larger mailing, but the Holy Spirit impressed upon me that as time went on I would be busier not less busy. The impression He made on me was that I would have many more stations. After my initial gasp and my questioning God as to how I could possible handle all the extra work and expenses, I gave in and placed my trust in Him.

Several months passed and even though I was faithful and tried marketing my shows, not one more T.V. station responded to my inquiries. I gradually drifted into taking it all upon myself again getting uptight thinking that God led me to do the show, and that I knew He wanted to use it to bring people closer to Him, so why wasn't He doing something; it didn't make sense to me. A minor, mental battle ensued over it after which I went before the Lord telling him that it was out of my hands; that I wasn't going to try to market the show anymore; that I was sorry that I couldn't bring in the audience that He deserved; that I would just work with my nine stations from then on in; I let it go.

Not long after that I attended a mission's conference in Massachusetts. After the morning session everyone had lunch in Fellowship Hall. I happened to sit at a farther wall where I could face everyone I had not seen in ages. God had it so that a pastor and his wife from Connecticut, whom I had heard about so many times, yet never met in person, sat across the table from me. I was dying to get into his area of Connecticut with my show; yet, I could not arrange to without a local sponsor. I held back from bombarding the pastor with a discussion about my show, and my request for sponsorship until I preceded my conversation with one of a more personal nature. After he finished eating I addressed my show with him. He agreed to sponsor me and to deliver my D.V.D.'s to the station in Connecticut; we exchanged information; that became my 10th station. God is so faithful.

THE REASON WHY

Do I think that God opened up the floodgates of heaven and poured out all the blessings I've written about because I'm a good kid? No, I do not. I believe that God and the Holy Spirit have a unique union, and that it pleases God, the Father, to produce the miracles and blessings that the Holy Spirit wishes for their children--us. We, God's children, are more instrumental than we realize in this process. If we are obedient to the third Person in the Holy Trinity; if we are faithful in prayer; if we ask believing that it was done in the finished work, then, yes, if the request will not hurt us, God will grant it in His timing.

Why was my life spared over 50 times? Why have my sons' lives been spared so many times? Why have they escaped injury so many times? Why has supernatural grace been so evident in all of my circumstances all through the years? Why is mercy always lying at my doorsteps? Why is God so evident in my life that even those looking in can see that I'm not making up anything, but that God continuously moves mountains?

Why does God orchestrate testimonies on a daily basis in my life rather than once every week or two? The answer is because He knows that I will be faithful to do something with them; that I will pass them on to edify the Body of Christ and not keep them to myself for my own edification.

Some people only have a relationship with the Holy Spirit; my church members and I have a fellowship with the Holy Spirit.

The measure of time we give to God is the measure of Himself that He gives back to us.

God will always expose a person's heart through the storms in his life. He reveals the nature and characteristics of our faith by what he has ordained to happen in the plan. God's people must be careful not to give into negativism when difficult times come along. Negativism challenges the record of God's kindness; it is clearly displayed in His Word. There is no need to analyze the past or question the future. Storms are a time for faith thoughts.

Three of my dear friends, after taking care of their grandchildren for many, many years, have been denied seeing the children again due to situations in their families. I cannot imagine anything more devastating. I know that the minutes turn into hours and hours into days and the days into weeks and months as these precious grandparents mourn for their loved ones. I know because I have experienced something quite similar. I know what it is like to cry my eyes out thinking that I would never see my loved ones again.

The reason I could stand by my friends and pray with such confidence for them is because God has proven to me that He is a God of reconciliation. He is a restorer of the breached. I have experienced this in my family and now we are whole. It did not happen overnight. I had to implement pure, unadulterated faith, the faith of Jesus Christ and to wait expectantly. Did the miracle happen without my involvement? No. I was a big part of God's plan for a blessed reunion; yet, I had to be highly sensitive to Him, not walking before Him. I also had to condescend to many concerned to follow the example of Jesus.

From my notes…Rather than waiting on God for a renewed mind, through faith, people try to bring situations to an end in the confines of their own ability, never living in the purpose of sovereignty…

KICKED LIKE A DOG

I was blessed with a visit from a friend I had not seen in over 15 years, and doubly blessed that she would actually drive for two hours to make the trip to my house. After our sweet reunion and an enjoyable lunch, we got comfortable on the two love seats in my living room where my friend who is 23 years younger began to pour out her heart about her past.

How could any woman go through so much? I wondered, as she related one event after another of sheer abuse. Listening to the terrible accounts of everything that happened in my friend's life brought back to my mind some of the awful treatment I had received during my lifetime, only her treatment was much worse. She had been beaten and (literally) kicked like a dog many times over, whereby my suffering was mainly emotional. She had been raped by a stranger producing not only a pregnancy, but a barrage of insults as if she were responsible for the crime.

How could someone with a background such as this come to a place where she has overcome all the negativity in her past life? Faith in God. How could someone, whose own mother cannot stand her due to circumstances surrounding her birth, rise above gross rejection? Faith in God. Once she gave it all over to God and stopped believing the lies that Satan told her about herself, she clothed herself with the Holy Spirit and with strength and confidence. She has exhibited mighty stamina to all who know her. Her children called her blessed. She secured employment of a high position, and she was given brand new opportunities. Many flock to her now for her words of encouragement and wisdom. How could all this happen? Faith in God.

I PRAYED FOR BOLDNESS

As a young believer I never possessed even the slightest amount of boldness to share Christ or my testimonies. I would tremble inside whenever I did. Strangely, when I participated with other church members in street evangelizing and passing out tracts, I was as free as a bird without any embarrassment or otherwise. Most certainly I was relying on the strength imparted to me by the saints in the group. For many years I asked God daily to cover me with the armor of God, which includes boldness, according to Ephesians 6:11-19. I did not pray that prayer ritualistically, nor did I pray it without activating faith; I prayed believing it would happen. I never stopped to evaluate myself to see if I had acquired it as the years went on, however.

In the winter of 2010, I became a Christian T.V. show host. To this day just before taping each show, I feel so incapable of doing the show that I want to crawl under something and hide. I feel nervous, insignificant, unknowledgeable, ugly and all the rest. 'I can't do this,' I tell myself. But then I lift my hands over my head and move them slowly from my head to my feet asking God to clothe me with the Holy Spirit. I pray for an anointing, boldness, confidence and for an audience of angels. The very moment when I ask Him to clothe me with the Spirit before I do my shows, He takes over; the transformation is instantaneous. I introduce myself and welcome my audience as if I have been doing it for 50 years. My friends tell me that I am a natural T.V. personality. I do not take any credit for this; It is all God; He is so faithful.

It would take volumes stretching from sea to shining sea to begin to reveal the faith of Jesus Christ to my readers. I have intentionally just skimmed the surface in order that my readers might grab onto a few tidbits.

CHAPTER 16

DREAMS

DRAWN TOGETHER LIKE MAGNETS

One night I woke up in the middle of the night dreaming that I had sudden eye contact with someone I knew and greatly respected. He was captured by me, and I by him. We were drawn to each other like magnets. We embraced. Our oneness and attraction had nothing to do with sensual love, but of a love that went far beyond earthly love. He slowly began to stride around the floor as he held me. Then I realized that my feet were on top of his feet like when I was a little girl dancing on my daddy's feet. He was gliding me across a room. It was then that I realized that it was the Lord. It intensifies the longing for Christ in a person's soul to wake up with dreams like this.

PREDICTION

I dream in colors; I always have. They say that one in 100 people dreams in colors. I do not believe this statistic is true because I put this out to my hundreds of Facebook friends and they responded by saying that most of them dream in colors. Anyway, I wonder what physical make-up determines if one dreams in colors...if any? I can't imagine dreaming in black and white. One night I dreamed that one of my sons brought me a fully cooked turkey dinner; everything was in bright colors---bright orange squash, white potatoes, light colored turkey, brown gravy. No wonder I am so full of life all the time. If my dreams were in black and white I would probably mope around.

FROLICKING

I woke up one time dreaming that I was frolicking in the water with church members at a beach when there was a run on fish-- mackerel, I think. We were suddenly surrounded by hundreds of fish. One third of the fish were dead and floating on top of the water. It was eerie having them floating all around us. I was either told or had the sense that someone would come to take away all the dead fish the following morning and so I felt better about it.

I'm wondering if all the dead fish represented the dead fish in our churches.

SO REALISTIC

I once dreamed of the last days and actually smelled chemicals in my dream. The smell was more atrocious than anything I had ever smelled. I believe the dream was a prediction, if not, why would I have dreamed it and even smelled the chemicals?

A FAVORITE

I dreamed that my friend, Sonny, left his keys with me for safe keeping. He left to go somewhere and told me that he wouldn't be long. The interpretation of this dream is that Sonny represents the Son of God,

Jesus. When he said that he wouldn't be long, that meant that Jesus wouldn't be long; in other words: He'll be coming soon in the rapture.

WIPER UPPER

I once dreamed that I was at a big church Body gathering like a convention, and a Body member spilled a big container of water all over many things and on the floor. I quickly got some paper towels and got down on my knees and began to wipe up the spill.

Interpretation: I think what God gave me pertaining to this dream is that it is my ministry to wipe up spills so to speak….spills of Body members, family, friends and acquaintances. This is my calling and I have been doing it for over 40 years.

I just love the way that God uses analogies in my dreams.

NINE MONTHS PREGNANT

5-13-2012--I dreamed that I was nine months pregnant and that I was being induced for delivery. As I dreamed it I was awakened at 3:30 in the morning, therefore I clearly remembered the dream.

Pregnancy in dreams always refers to something new---a new path etc. The dream was indicative of something brand new that would happen in my life.

In my a.m. devotional a few hours later, the Spirit of God revealed to me in two portions of Scripture that He was about to do something big in my life. He always backs up dreams with Scripture. That is why the title of this book is 'Radical Rapport'.

TWINS

And again---another new life dream. I dreamed that I had twin baby girls, and that the newborn baby girls actually crawled. Not only did the dream depict something new about to happen, the twins in the dream depicted a double blessing in the new thing that would take place in my life.

This prediction came true within one year. During the nine months that I packed my belongings to move, and while I was waiting to be led of God concerning my moving, my pastor and church family prayed every, single Sunday morning at our church breakfast that God would open some type of ministry in Brunswick where I was headed. They were prayers of faith and rest because we knew that we knew that God was going to do something big and something wonderful.

Two months after I moved, God gave us (the church members and me) full definition as to what He wanted to accomplish at my new place of residence. My church has been allowed to use the community room in my housing complex for Christian mini-concerts every month. Because the gospel message to us is more important than music, we present Scripture, testimonies, prayer and encouragement in between songs. The concerts are very popular and well attended.

So yes, the get-togethers are the new life that God predicted in my dreams. And yes, they are a double blessing as the twin babies in my dream portrayed.

WHATEVER DID THIS DREAM MEAN?

I dreamed on 4-3-12 that a friend's wife died and that he and I got married simply for companionship. We slept separately and simply shared a house. I had a tremendous need for individuality and independence after being divorced for over 20 years and living alone, although I had a need for company; yet, was challenged by all the guests that filled all the rooms of the house all the time in the dream. One of the reasons for all the company was because I was deceived into thinking

pg. 173

that if I busied myself with visitors, I would not be a nuisance to my new husband whom I presumed would want some space from me.

He was a very quiet man and I could tell that he was worn out from all the company and from suppressing his feelings in order to respect me. One day he walked through our big house and plopped on the couch sort of expressionless. For the first time since we were joined in marriage, my heart was enlarged for him, and I left a stack of coffee cups from serving my company and sauntered over to the couch and gently lay beside him to comfort him from his heartbreak. I was taken back when he responded to my gesture by grabbing a hold of a big blanket and throwing it over the both of us as he embraced me. I instantly woke up. I will never forget how wonderful it felt. I perceived that this man represented Jesus.

One of the interpretations could be that we must make time for God in the middle of our social lives.

MY GRANDMOTHER

For 40 years of my life I wondered if my maternal grandmother made it to heaven. As a young believer I remembered her as being a hard, foul-mouthed immigrant who drank excessively. I had never heard her mention God except in taking His name in vain. Neither did she cry out for God on her death bed in the convalescent home, but for my grandfather who had passed many years beforehand. I thought for sure that she would spend eternity in the deep abyss.

My thoughts changed as I grew in faith, however, and I began to wonder as to my grandmother's life before she left Italy to come to America with my grandfather and her sisters----bitter/sweet for sure. The separation from her parents and the rest of her family certainly had to cause her loneliness and severe depression. I began to think about the hush-hush stories I had heard when I became a teenager and my ears were in tuned to such things---stories of my grandfather abusing her physically and mentally after drinking himself drunk after work every day.

I began to think that my grandmother probably turned to God many times back then and that maybe, just maybe, she had a deep love for God as a child. I may have turned to alcohol to fix my hurts too if I didn't become one of His? In time I began to realize that I judged wrongly all the distasteful things she did which included swearing at us kids and being mean and nasty so much of the time.

My grandfather too had his reasons for turning to alcohol. His entire family was buried alive in hot lava as Mount Vesuvius in southern Italy exploded spewing out burning ash all through the nearby towns. I never questioned his eternal salvation as I had my grandmother's eternal salvation though because he was always loving us up; my thinking was so immature.

Well, everyone has heard me say over and over that God has saved the best for last, and that He has blessed my senior years exceedingly more than He blessed my young and middle- aged years. He did it again in the form of a dream He gave me about my grandmother. As I relate this dream keep in mind that there was no way I could possibly have conjured up a dream of this sort.

I dreamed that I was in heaven and I met my grandmother. She was filled with the Holy Spirit of God and abundant praises to Him flowed from her lips. My mother was off to the side watching the happy event. I approached my grandmother to try to tell her who I was when I was deliriously surprised to hear her speaking my language- English. A delightful conversation ensued. We were both filled with glory.

Often, I do not remember my dreams upon awakening; yet, I remembered everything clearly that time as it seemed that I was experiencing more of a heart vision than having a dream. I woke up believing that my grandmother was in the presence of God. I believe that hearing her speak the same language as me was indicative of her speaking God's heavenly language, and that she is one of the Lord's. God in His goodness chose to save some really special blessings until the time of my life when I would need them most. I am so thankful that His ways are not our ways.

MY DAD

I once dreamed of my (earthly) father in heaven whereby he looked at me very lovingly saying directly, 'you are still in my household'.

The only thing I could think of the next morning when I prayed about a meaning was that at one point when he was alive he was so upset about my Christianity and the ministry I was in that he threatened to take me out of his will; not that he didn't believe in God, it was just that my becoming born- again was so 'far out' from the way everyone in our family was raised.

Maybe my father wanted me to know that he relented of his displeasure in me since the truth was revealed to him in heaven.

MY MOTHER

And there was the dream I had of my mother in which she was adorning me with beautiful, shiny blouses with beautiful designs on them. One appeared to be too big for me, yet she assured me that I would fit into it.

I do not believe that this dream had to do with my earthly mother, but my spiritual Mother, the Holy Spirit. I believe that my early mother in the dream depicted the Holy Spirit. I believe that God, the Holy Spirit was showing me in my dream what He was doing in my life---adorning me with beauty---clothing me with His beautiful life. I believe that when I said in the dream that I thought a certain blouse would be too big for me, that it was symbolic of what I had been saying to Him for months which was that I was nervous about going nationwide or even worldwide with the ministry He had given me. The Spirit assuring me in my dream that I would fit into the blouse referred to me being able to take on a much bigger audience---with His help, of course.

It behooves me that so many people would close their eyes to this language; to me it is a gift of God. It would be impossible for any person to conjure up dreams like this with a spiritual connotation.

RECURRING DREAM

Although this is a recurring dream the people and images differ. I am a trip organizer in the dream. My church members and I are getting ready to fly to heaven in a plane. It is my responsibility to make sure that each person has his/her ticket and luggage. I could see myself clearly going from one person to the next to the next checking their papers.

The dream is self explanatory; it depicts what I do in life--remind others to prepare their hearts to meet the Lord.

EXCHANGING GIFTS

In one of my dreams my pastor and I were exchanging gifts. I believe the pastor represented God in the dream; it was self-explanatory.

ADAMS STREET

Adams Street was located three streets away from where I lived in Bridgeport, Connecticut growing up. To Christians the word adam represents man. So why would the word adam be significant to me in my dream? The reason is that adam speaks of our being in the natural man as opposed to being in the Spirit, and so the Holy Spirit used the dream of my being on Adams Street to convey to me that I was in adam (my human nature) which could mean that I had been lax in my faith, or that I committed inadvertent sin in my life. With the interpretation of that dream, I would trace my words and actions of the preceding days to discover my negligence or my error, repent of whatever it was, and go on.

How faithful of the Holy Spirit, Who, with the other two parts of the Trinity, to bother with a human being like me, to put me in check to transform me, one incident at a time, to be more like Jesus.

CHAPTER 17

GRACE

MANY MEANINGS

This is not original with me, but I love it: At the table of grace the cup is never empty, the plate is always full and it's never too late. I also love the term 'radical grace' because it goes along with God's 'radical rapport' with us.

To be absolved from discipline instead of getting what we deserve can fall into the lines of grace as well as mercy, I think. When we do or say something wrong and we and God are the only ones that know about the sin, and we could easily be found out, and God covers the wrong so that nobody finds out, it is a paramount example of His divine favor: grace. When we are in a conversation and we are on the verge of saying something that ultimately may incriminate us, and the Holy Spirit prompts someone else to add to the conversation before we get a chance to voice what is on the tip of our tongue; God is sparing us embarrassment or possibly shame. This is His divine favor: grace. He justifies us through His divine process.

Grace is so far from law that we, in our finite minds, cannot begin to conceive of a distance that great. Grace is always available to us. Even when we slip away from grace, we can reclaim it. All we need to do is to rebound when we fall; confess our iniquities and ask for grace. It is not that grace gives us a license to sin, but when we do sin grace covers us.

WE MUST COMPREHEND THAT! WE MUST ASK FOR A REVELATION OF GRACE IN ORDER TO BEGIN TO COMPREHEND IT. We cannot simply possess a blasé or ho hum attitude toward something as wonderful as God's grace. Grace sets us free. Who doesn't want to be free from everything that tries to hinder us?

Grace produces awe in our daily lives. Personally, it gives me fresh motivation to write on the days I do not feel like writing. It gives me an overflow of fresh thoughts to write about when my mind is all dried up; that is how amazing grace is. When the devil exchanges God's truth for lies, grace, in a matter of a fraction of a second, gives power back to truth. When I hear strange noises while on my bed at night, grace calms my fears. When I am having an infrequent nightmare, He wakes me out of it before something horrible happens, right in the nick of time; I view that as grace.

God brings enemies in to reveal an unbelieving heart not vertically oriented to grace. It is not what God sends that reveals who I am; it is that I reveal who I am through what God sends. God will bring out of me what is within me.

God treats us so wonderfully, as kings and priests, even though we are so undeserving. This is grace…

Grace transforms…

Grace is unending…

We all have grace in our lives in multi-faceted ways. We do not deserve it, and we give it to others who do not deserve it from us. When we give others Christ instead of giving them what they deserve, we are giving them grace. In plain English--when people make negative comments at my Facebook site assuming that they know who I am, which they don't, and I feel like setting them straight with an attitude-- I don't. I overpower the natural with the spiritual. I come back with an answer that is filled with grace.

Grace always abounds. Grace comes in waves. When my brother was dying and I was scared to watch him take his last breath, grace abounded and calmed my fears turning an unpleasant event into a wonderful experience where I was surrounded by angels.

The hundreds of times I was down on myself God manifested His grace in numerous, unique ways. One time, in particular, I was unable to forgive myself about something. It just happened to be the Sunday that my friend David gave the intro at church. What did he speak on?... giving ourselves grace. That is dreadfully difficult to do, but it is what God implores us to learn to do. This grace keeps coming; it is inexhaustible. This is such a comforting thought.

 From my notes: God's grace will never go where God's will doesn't take us…

Grace leads us to mercy…

It is through grace that God gives us blessings….

Grace is our teacher…these four words encapsulate volumes of heavenly language…

We stand in the grace of God. I have been enveloped in grace in each of mine and my sons' close calls to death, injuries and mishaps through the years numbering into the hundreds. It was God's grace that had somebody return my lost manuscript to me after I had worked on it for several months and lost it while traveling. When my marriage ended after 30 years, it was only the grace of God that kept me sane and able to function. It was God's grace that kept me from going hungry for years when I didn't earn enough money to pay all my bills and to buy much food. When I took care of my aging mother for two months at a time in a two room apartment in which she awakened me all through the nights, it was only God's grace that kept me from cracking up. It was God's grace that led me to sing a song at church one day that would keep someone in the building from committing suicide that very afternoon as she had planned because of the death of her only child. It was God's grace that enabled me to go to work every day with a busted back, and His grace that kept me when I would have to lean over my patients' beds to give them bed baths when my pain would produce tears, and when I had to lift them into their wheelchairs. Grace, grace marvelous grace…

The application of grace from divine viewpoint cannot be limited by sin, because grace paid for sin and there is nothing it can do against grace. If sin abounds, grace will much more abound. Is grace a license to sin? God forbid, but if we do, His grace is sufficient. The purpose of grace is to lead us into repentance from wrong thinking. If only the entire Christian population would take a little time to meditate on what grace involves.

Thank You, Lord, for Your indescribable, beautiful, matchless, wonderful, amazing grace.

AMAZING GRACE

Even though I write six days a week, Monday is the day when I delve into my work more resolutely than any other day. I am still reeling from the weekend and from hearing Sunday morning's sermon and spending time with church members. I produce my T.V. show in the morning and record the notes I wrote down at church. Everything is fresh in my mind and thoughts come to me at the speed of lightning. It is an effort for me to leave the keyboard and even to take time for meals.

If I happen to have an appointment or something else scheduled for a Monday, it puts a slight damper on my day and I am not as productive. But, one particular Monday was entirely different, extremely constructive. I finished my show bright and early; I went to the motor vehicle office to get a duplicate copy of my driver's license; I treated myself to lunch at a restaurant I had never been to before enjoying the most delectable fried haddock and home cut fries, plus I had mouth watering chocolate creme pie for dessert; I went to the store where I buy hard candies cheap and bought my monthly stash. When I returned home I accomplished an immense amount of writing and then I relaxed and watched a movie.

Half way through the movie I put it on pause and made a phone call to try to locate an old friend who seemed to have disappeared off the face of the earth. I was able to reach someone who knew of her whereabouts. The person related to me that my friend's daughter had to put her in a home because she had dementia and was to the stage that she was hurting herself and needed supervision. The news was so disturbing to me that my heart grieved with heaviness. My friend had waited for years to enjoy the first home of her own, and just a few months after she realized her dream she took a turn for the worst. I could hardly bear the thoughts of her being in a nursing facility and homesick.

As devastating as the news was to me, God showed me that He arranged a special day of fulfillment and incredible blessings for me by His grace as the grace was padding for me to receive and bear the sad news. I knew that His grace would continue to hold me up through the remaining hours of the evening.

HE SAVED MY PHONE AND KEYS

I headed to the Laundromat in my complex before 7 a.m. one brisk morning donning a winter coat for the first time of the season. After locking the front door I placed my key ring with my house and car keys along with my cell phone in my coat pocket. As I walked down the walkway I noticed my keys sticking out through the bottom of my coat. I reached into my pocket to discover that there was a big hole. I was in shock thinking about how many times I could have lost my keys and phone; yet, because of God's grace it did not happen. Had it happened my woes would have been compounded because my pocketbook with my spare keys was inside my apartment; I would have been locked out.

My heart was overwhelmed with thanksgiving to the Lord as I was reminded of when my gold cross necklace, a gift from my parents in the 50's, was dangling from the floor of my car half out the car door when I noticed it one time in the early 90's. How it got there I will never know, but if it ever fell completely to the ground and I did not notice it (and that was an immense possibility because the parking lot where I parked was always heavy with traffic,) I would never have gotten over it.

I instinctively knew that there had to be hundreds, if not thousands, of similar incidents in my life's experience whereby God poured His grace upon me sparing me from all sorts of things. Lord, help me to reflect on Your goodness more often.

~~~~~~~~~~~~~~~~~~~~~~~~~~~~~

It would take volumes reaching from the Atlantic to the Pacific to begin to touch on God's grace. I have intentionally just skimmed the surface in order that these few tidbits might stay with my readers.

pg. 182

CHAPTER 18

GOD'S VOICE

I LOVE HIS VOICE

God spoke creation into existence. His voice is powerful and majestic; at the same time it is soft and sweet.

Who tells the sun the exact time of its setting? Who appoints the moon for the seasons? The great designer of the universe...that's Who.

Our God is the designer of designers. Evidence of this is found in many portions of the Old Testament. A portion from Ezekiel 27 tells of planks and boards from fir trees from Senir, a peak of Mt. Hermon being used for a project that God was designing, not just any old planks and boards but those specific ones. Another portion tells of cedars from Lebanon that were used to make a mast and of the oaks of Basham that were used to make oars. A deck and benches were made of boxwood from the coasts of Cyprus inlaid with ivory.

The Bible tells how that fine linen with embroidered work from Egypt was used to make a sail—blue-purple from the coasts of Elisha (of Asia Minor) was the ship's awning. God has always had a divine design in mind for His purposes, and He speaks those things into being through His people.

Job 33:19 tells us that God's voice may be heard by man when he is chastened with pain upon his bed and with continued strife in his home. The variety of ways that God uses His voice is numerous.

The Book of Song of Solomon in the Bible tells us that when we are sleeping our heart is awake. And it is through our heart being awake in the night season that God speaks to us. When I awake in the morning it is not exactly a new beginning of a new day; it is a continuation of my heart being with my heavenly Lover during the night when my physical body slept. Remnants of dreams and my being in the presence of God during the night play over and over causing me to reel in the same manner anyone would reel after watching a performance and leaving a Broadway play or an opera house.

VOICE OR TEXT?

As much as I hate texting, when my youngest son was sick in bed and bored for three days and texted me a few times each day, I became instantly aware that reading his messages instead of hearing his voice caused the messages to by-pass my head and to go directly to my heart. My senses were heightened and I received his communication much more intently than I would have had he communicated with me with his voice. Meditation on God followed. I heard God say that His reasoning for choosing to communicate with His children through written words rather than to talk to us with His audible voice is because of that exact reason. Invariably, we would take Him for granted if we heard His audible voice telling us that He loves us, and giving us directions for our journey of faith. It simply would not be the same.

The following day at church the Holy Spirit directed my pastor's message toward me regarding needing a breakthrough in my ministries--- T.V. and public speaking. What the Spirit said to me was that if God had given me direction with His voice, I would have taken His voice for granted; but, by speaking to me through his chosen vessel in the Body of Christ, the communication was going straight to my heart and not to my mind. It also made me appreciate the uniqueness of God to minister to me according to my own make-up.

HE NAILED IT

I remember being under a stronghold due to a problem in my family. I lay on my couch watching Christian T.V. A host was on who I never heard before, and he had guests on whom I had never seen before. I was under tremendous emotional pressure at that hour concerning a family member. These words concerning that family member went through my mind: 'You are killing me'. Exactly one minute later the host of the show said that his friend told his kid: 'You are killing me'; you are going put me in my grave. It was as if the guy on T.V. was right next to me and looking inside my head; ultimately it was God speaking to me.

I went to the Bible and opened at random to a portion in the Book of Jeremiah which spoke about a stronghold on the daughter of my people. His message to me could not have been any clearer; there was, in fact, a stronghold on me.

As soon as I recognized it, I renounced it, and the victory was the Lord's.

COULD IT BE?

Through a multitude of years I have endured severe back pain; yet, I made a calculated decision not to pray for healing even though I knew full well that God had the power to heal me if He chose. Then the time came after the condition worsened to an unbearable stage when I thought maybe I was not in His will by refusing to ask for healing, so just to cover all the bases I started to pray for a healing.

This is simply speculative, but I am wondering if the reason God has not chosen to heal me from my back condition is because He has a tremendous amount of work for me to do from the confines of my bedroom/office, and if I did not have physical limitations I would be traveling and gallivanting all over the place giving Him and His work only some of my time rather than all of it. So maybe when I complete all my tasks which include more books and a screen play, then He will surprise me.

Just sayin…

AN AHA MOMENT

Omgosh! I found this note an hour after I wrote the above story: 'It was the fact that Mephibosheth was lame that kept him at the king's table.' I am speechless! The Lord hath spoken. His voice could not have been clearer. I have a condition, yet I am seated at the King's table.

HIS VOICE IN A DREAM

And there was the night when I dreamed that I was in a high school and went into the principal's office. He mentioned to me that I had seen the movie, 'Secretariat', two times. I immediately knew that He was God and that He knew everything about me. Upon awakening I recalled the dream and came to the realization that, I did, indeed, see the movie, 'Secretariat', two times. I was not aware of any revelation of the dream; it was interesting just the same.

A DISCIPLINARY TONE

There is a verse in the book of Jeremiah which reads: 'You see yourself with too flattering an eye to detect your guilt.' God usually gives me this verse when I am off on something, and I am, indeed, looking at myself (my opinions) with too flattering an eye. It is no different than if He were standing next to me speaking the words.

IT'S ALL HIM

After boxing rounds with God (in the same way that Jacob wrestled with Him,) telling Him, "No, I can't get any additional T.V. stations; my inquiries fall on deaf ears", to "O.K. I will try harder to get on more stations", something interesting happened:

I was led to turn on Christian T.V. late one night. Here we go again---a preacher with whom I had a difficult time listening to because I did not agree with the doctrine that he preached was preaching. I wanted to change the channel, but God wouldn't let me. Within one minute of my turning on the T.V. (the message from God always comes within a minute, not five or ten minutes,) he shared a story about when God first called him into the ministry many years earlier. God led him to rent space to have a church service. To his knowledge there were only seven chairs in the room. The Spirit of God spoke to him and told him where to find a hundred chairs and told him to set them up. Along with those words God told him that he had been faithful in the small ministry He had given him at first, and that it was time for Him to enlarge the size of his ministry.

I knew that it was not a coincidence that God led me into the living room to turn on the T.V. that night because all I ever watch on T.V. is the news and I rarely watch T.V. late at night. So there it was: you have been faithful in a little (10 T.V. stations), so now I will increase your number.

HE NEVER SAID NO

I went to my friend Bev's Bible study in Lewiston, Maine one morning. All the women were talking about some man they knew who never said 'no'. They told about how he was always helping people and that he never did it grudgingly. As they shared about him arranging work for the unemployed, and doing multiple favors for everybody, I perked up inside and realized that I too never say 'no'. I had been venting to my close friend about never being able to catch my breath with the constant requests that come to me on a daily basis, only I did some of my stuff grudgingly; I felt a twinge of shame.

The more the women talked, the more the Spirit of God began to reveal to me the following: I didn't know the man they spoke of, but I wished I could have known him. I loved hearing about him. I wanted to be just like him and have the angels talk to each other about how she never says 'no'.

Thanks ladies for sharing stories about that man and for giving me food for thought.

MY SCHEDULE

You may wonder at first what this next story is doing in this chapter, but you will get the connection after you read a few paragraphs...

My schedule in addition to housework includes personal care, appointments, shopping, pharmacy, laundry, cooking, recyclables, banking, doing bills and paperwork, studying, writing and producing a T.V. show, burning dozens of discs every month and doing a huge mailing to T.V, stations, updating my blogs, correspondence, meetings, writing books (and a screenplay), coordinating and advertising concerts, involvement in church activities, greeting card ministry, social events, making videos of many of the events and burning them to discs, entertaining company and keeping in touch by phone with at least three dozen people that I have to call weekly, bi-weekly or monthly---aunts, uncles, cousins, elderly people and family members; and those things do not include the unexpected. And I should mention that I am on an ice pack a lot as I accomplish these tasks, and I am often on ice while driving around doing my errands.

Winter brings with it the responsibility of cleaning the snow off my car and removing it so that management can plow and treat the roads. If the cars are not immediately removed they will be towed. This occurrence takes place on an average of two times a week from December to March. The garbage shacks where I live are at the end of the road so they are not as handy as I would like. Laundry must be done at the Laundromat on the premises as there are no washers or dryers in the units. What all this adds up to is that even as seniors we don't get a chance to slow down; the workload is constant.

And just like in households across America, computer problems play havoc at least four times a year. Getting zapped with unexpected expenses is another curve ball. Having to incorporate a regiment of exercises into an already full schedule after weeks of physical therapy has been virtually impossible.

One day it really caught up to me. I was supposed to squeeze in laundry between a dentist visit and company. I ended up cleaning out the refrigerator and washing a sink load of dishes too. I was so weak that I just had to rest and clear my mind. Without God I would have been as wrung out as a wet dish rag, but because God's grace is so beneficial a few minutes of rest brought resurrection. I was filled with energy and anticipation. I entertained company; I ended up accomplishing two days work in one evening and even squeezed in a movie. Asking God to establish our steps in the morning, the way the Bible says, makes all the difference. People have offered to help me, and if I thought I couldn't handle it, I would accept their offers, but until God tells me to, I will go it alone. Moses was told by his counterparts to spread out his workload amongst others, but that was not God's perfect will. The secret for me has been to abide in His grace moment by moment (and more recently second by second), and not to be swayed from it. "I can do all things through Christ that strengthens me".

The next day I read in Isaiah 40 that God is not a weary God. In Isaiah 30:30-31 it reads, "And the Lord will cause His glorious voice to be heard and the descending blow of his arm to be seen, coming down with indignant anger and with the flame of a devouring fire, amid crashing blast and cloudburst, tempest and hailstones. At the voice of the Lord the Assyrians will be stricken with dismay and terror, while He smites them with His rod". This is not an uplifting portion of Scripture; yet, it brings out clearly the power in the voice of God. He reiterated it for me, personally, through these passages.

PUBLISH

Isaiah 30:8… "Now go and inscribe this on a tablet…write it in a book". I can't tell you how many times God has spoken to me through this verse.

HE PUT THE CAT ON THE TABLE

Then there was the time, between sleep and wakefulness, when I heard the voice of God. "Bette-Jean: why do you always have to be in charge?" He asked. I was taken back at God's sternness and also at what He said. "What?" I was astonished and taken back, not only to hear His voice, but at what He asked me, that I responded to Him in the same way I would have responded to a family member, in a common tone.

God could not have picked a better time to get my attention. In those moments of the morning when my head is uncluttered, undisturbed and unimaginably clear, I am closer to God than in all the moments and hours that follow. I immediately began to analyze my actions of a few days prior. Whether I understood anything or not, I knew that God knew way more about me than I knew about myself, and I wanted to change my ways whatever they may have been. He spoke to me tenderly and gave me glimpses into areas of my life that needed to be changed in order for me to grow to be like Him. In instructing me He showed me that listening to His Spirit on most everything was good, but He wanted me to go beyond listening to some things, to checking out everything with Him --all things even when and how I performed seemingly menial tasks. Lesson learned.

PERSONAL PRONOUNS

I was planning to put my car in the auto body shop to have my fender damage repaired after I was in an accident. I made a list of projects that I would tackle during the time that I would be confined to my house. They included: switching summer and winter clothes; digging out pictures to hang in my apartment; baking a fresh peach pie; darning socks the old fashioned way; calling the computer geeks; doing laundry; working on my manuscript, marketing, producing my T.V. show and more.

I had to have the car at the shop at 8:00 a.m. and the owner would give me a ride home. I was most anxious to get started on my list of projects, and as soon as I got out of bed thoughts ran through my mind of which project I would tackle first. I have always welcomed the opportunities to be confined to the house even in snow storms as these times afford me mega opportunities to catch up on projects that I put off. I took my morning pill, spent time with God in prayer and then proceeded to read my Bible. The first portion that God gave me was Job Chapter 29. I was bombarded with a bunch of little, yellow highlighted spots on the page, and knew instantly what was before me without even having to read a word. It was the chapter about Job being into himself; the chapter where 50 pronouns-I, me and my- were used in his defending himself before the Lord.

What that said to me was that the personal pronoun, I, described me that morning. Did I give my every second to God and ask Him to establish my steps before I entertained those thoughts about which project I would tackle first? No, I didn't. And He was letting me know it--graciously, I might add.

Only a few weeks had gone by since God had spoken to me about wanting to be in control, and I again slipped into myself before I gave him my thoughts that morning. It's not a condemning thing at all so don't get me wrong; if God did not put me in check the way He does, one little stray would lead to two and two little strays would lead to three and so on until I would lose my sensitivity to Him altogether. I totally get that and thank Him so much for loving me so much that He would extend me the kindness.

GIVE A CLEARING OF YOURSELF

An incident occurred which concerned me and a friend of mine. It wasn't an actual problem--just something that was weighing on me. Even though I wanted to bring it to light, I didn't want to make waves in the friendship. The way I left it with God was that if she brought it up I would tell her everything that was on my heart.

pg. 191

She did not bring it up.

The following morning during my pastor's message, he kept making statements such as: give a clearing of yourself; give a defense; give an answer that's inside your heart; set things straight. He went on to say that by doing these things we may release the other party from un-needed weight. Those statements were a rhema to me regarding what God wanted me to do in the situation. Could He be any more direct!

The following morning I private messaged the person and explained everything to her. I ended the message by telling her that I knew it would be 'all good' with her. She wrote back to thank me and ended her message by telling me that it was 'all good' with her.

God's way is the only way that makes any sense.

MY PROOF-READER

Often, when I am lying in bed meditating before I get out of bed in the morning, the Holy Spirit puts information in my mind pertaining to books or projects that I am working on to alert me that I have made an omission or an error, or to give me additional words or thoughts to add onto my work. When He does this it truly blows me away for each is something I would never have thought of on my own.

THE SOFTEST VOICE EVER

On 10-25-2013 I heard an audible voice say: "Jesus is coming"…

CHAPTER 19

FAMILY AND FRIENDS

A GODLY INSTITUTION

…I could not have made it through life without the love of family…

Only God could have thought of designing a family. Aloneness is not a good thing. How else would people know how to share with others? Even if family members are not particularly close, something inside us tells us that inherent love in our parents, siblings and relatives overpowers all else, and that they would always be there for us at least in thought.

During the times in my life when I had been the loneliest; the times when I was miles away on my own; one syllable, not even a complete phone call or sentence, but just one syllable from one of my sons' voices would instantly melt my heart and produce tears; that is the mighty power of God's love; it is beyond explanation.

MY SONS

Most mothers would give their eye teeth for a baby girl, but I thank God always for my boys. I am what you call a 'boy person'. My boys were easy to raise and outdoorsy from the get go. They never complained about having to wear hand-me-downs. They never complained about having to bake their own snacks, and to sew their own buttons on their shirts when my hectic workload would not permit me to do mending at times. They never complained about having to work digging clams to buy their school clothes before they reached the age of ten; they were ecstatic to have jobs. They all did their chores dutifully since they were little tots of three---my little soldiers. To them it was a privilege to stand on a chair to wash dishes and to play with the soap suds at the age of five. Mommy allowing them to make their own peanut butter and jelly sandwiches at age five, to them, was to them like flying on a magic carpet.

Sure, they gave me a run for my money in their teenage years, but considering the horror stories I have heard over the years about the relationships between mothers and daughters---paleeze---give me my boys.

Manhood matured them even though they were young men long before their biological years caught up with them. Adulthood has transformed them inwardly to intelligent, caring and nurturing human beings; I can leave this world in peace.

My physical body may not be very big, yet the size of my heart is out of proportion to the rest of me. It would take the body of a giant to contain it because my children's love has so drastically enlarged it; they would do anything for me.

Tony, George, Gary and Corey…my four wonderful sons…I love you.

FAMILY VISITS

Whether it is a yearly visit from Tony and Tracie, or Corey stopping in or taking me out for dinner when he is in Maine every few months or so, or George and Sandy or Gary and Brenda stopping in, I get to play the mommy role again bringing me untold joy. I don't realize how much I miss it until they are in my home. I hope they experience the same feelings when I visit them. I know so many people without closeness with their kids, and that makes my relationship with my kids even more special. That doesn't mean that we agree on everything or anything like that, it just means that we are family; they belong to me and I belong to them. They will never know until eternity the important role they have played in my life.

BREAKFAST WITH THE KIDS

Often on a Saturday morning I will get a call from my son and daughter-in-law inviting me to breakfast at a popular, local restaurant. These spontaneous invites are like a shot in the arm. The atmosphere is bustling and warm; the surroundings pleasant and inviting; the food splendid. These are the times in which we catch up--face to face, not over the phone or via e-mail.

GRANDS

My grandchildren total nine in all with my firstborn T.J. being in heaven waiting for the rest of us to join him.

It is so joyful to stand back and to watch how my grandkids have grown from children to adults and to make a mental evaluation of how they have fared in life--not without trials and temptations, but overcoming the troubles that have bombarded them. They are all hard workers, family oriented and good at what they do. Forgive me if I am boasting. Each one along with each spouse is a gift from God.

Ever since I lived in Maryland for just shy of 10 years, I have had a surrogate granddaughter, Jasmine, who lives there. We did things together when she was a teenager. I have missed her since moving back to Maine, but with the Internet we are able to keep in touch. Thank You, God, and thank you Mark Zuckerberg.

GREAT-GRANDS

My great-grandchildren number 13 in all. The gatherings and visits with them are infrequent, yet very special. These youngsters bless me to pieces. When we are together, judging from all the kisses and hugs, they love their Nana. They are all such good kids and their parents are doing such a fine job with them that I can't help but be proud. The intelligence of kids today blows my mind, and being in their presence is startling and entertaining. As modern and as smart as they are though, I make sure that I set up an old fashioned tea party on my coffee table with a pitcher filled with pretend tea (water) and cups, spoons and cookies for little Aaliyah when she visits. These occasional festivities warm my heart, plus I hope she remembers them when she grows up.

MY SISTER'S E-MAILS

Keeping in touch with my sister, Vicki, via e-mail a few times every week is so good for my soul. Because I moved away from our hometown many years ago I don't know what is going on amidst acquaintances; therefore, she keeps me up to date. She also sends me photos of all her family events for which I can't thank her enough. Her husband, Nick, sometimes posts photos for me too. I know I wouldn't be the happy person I am if these photos didn't keep coming. I am so thankful to God for modern technology.

AUNTIE B.J.

I have been blessed with the most amazing niece and nephew, their spouses, great niece and great-nephews ever. They have been exceedingly faithful in keeping in touch with me through the years with phone calls, e-mails, notes, pictures, Facebook posts and surprise packages in the mail. The respect that they show me is inferior to no respect ever shown a person. My life would not be the same without them in it.

My Ethiopian girlfriend's daughters have been calling me Auntie B.J. all their lives. Now that they are older and using Google it is so joyful to have them not only call me on the phone, but to contact me through the Internet.

RELATIVES

It is a blessing to come from two large families, one on my mother's side and one on my father's side. Through the years my relatives and I have kept fairly close even though everyone is scattered throughout the United Sates. We have become closer still through the social networks--distant relatives also-- making life that much nicer. This may sound overstated, but communicating with all of them makes me even more cognizant of their blood flowing through my veins. We may only see one another at funerals, or we may never see one another anymore; yet, the fragrance of memory can transform us, in a split second, to when we were kids, and our thoughts can take us, ever so briefly, into a magic kingdom that by far surpasses Disneyworld.

My uncle, approaching 90, still has the intelligence of a 20 year old. He has always been a brain, very knowledgeable with ham radios and high intelligence stuff. He was an asset to the United States military during wartime. He lives in Colorado. He still tells me fascinating stories about when he was in the war.

I thank God for all my aunts, uncles, cousins, second cousins and all their families.

JOAN

Joan has been my faithful friend since our sons were little and in cub scouts. We worked at a health club together; we worshiped together, and she drove me to Canada a few times to catch flights overseas via an airport there. She was the only one who wrote to me when I was out of the country. She also helped me to re-locate when I moved to Maryland introducing me to her aunt who lived nearby in Baltimore City. We have gone out for lunch and dinner numerous times over the years. She is always bringing me stuff--oranges from Florida, pizza stuffers from the Italian restaurant, healthy snacks and you name it. When I go to her house she always makes me a healthy salad. She is a true confidant. I cannot imagine my life without her. Thank You, Lord, for giving me Joan.

MY CUBAN FRIENDS

My friends in Cuba who I met in the 90's while on the mission field have added greatly to my life. Our correspondence is not as frequent as it used to be, yet we will always be very much a part of one another's hearts. When they became grandparents for the first time, it was as if I had become a grandparent for the first time. Only God could ordain a meaningful friendship like this.

Pavel was my Spanish professor overseas. We rarely connect these days only intermittently through a social media, yet he is a part of my heart. His love is a love that someone has for family. It is satisfying to have the same heartbeat as someone who thinks of you as family. His friendship has greatly benefitted my life.

I cherish the memory of all my Cuban friends and former neighbors. They are in my thoughts and prayers always.

MY PRECIOUS DAUGHTER

After being on Facebook for over four years and receiving thousands of comments on my wall, the strangest thing happened. One day I accessed my page as usual and there was not one comment or message posted. Even stranger was the absence of posts and comments the following day and two days later. It had been customary for me to get six comments from friends every morning, comments that I looked forward to as they blessed me abundantly.

On the third day I felt a sharp pain in my heart because of the profound absence of their correspondence in my life. The devil tried to put some negative thoughts in my head concerning the situation, but the Holy Spirit overpowered him with this thought: Certainly it could not be a coincidence. God had to be teaching me something. He connected with my spirit and said that this would be the start of a new season for me. I accepted it. Although the cessation of my friends' comments would be a tremendous loss, a bitter pill to swallow, I was determined not to dwell in pity. I would instead embrace the new season to which God was takikng me.

'When God closes a door, He always opens a window,' and that is precisely what God did for me in the days that followed my blank Facebook page. I received a message from a Facebook friend, Colleen, who I had come to know and love deeply through the network. She is one of the most amazing women of God that I have ever known. She had shared with me through our occasional correspondence how lonely she was for family. Quite casually one day she mentioned that she would love to have me for a grandmother. Well, I knew how old she was and I wasn't old enough to be her surrogate grandmother, but God began to stir my heart to pour out His love to her through me, and in so doing to receive His love to me through her, so I wrote her back and said: 'I already have a surrogate granddaughter, but I could use a surrogate daughter.'

Colleen's response to my note blew me away. She was excited and happy. I imagined her to be jumping for joy. Come to find out, she is the same age that the baby girl I lost in pregnancy in the early 60's would have been...within five months. So God gave this child of God who had longings that only He knew about, a spiritual mother, and He gave me a spiritual daughter. Our kindred spirits have blessed us beyond what we could have asked or thought.

When God is getting ready to bring something wonderful into our lives He usually introduces us first to some type of pain; in my case it was heart pain. The size of our pain is a clue to the size of our blessing. The spiritual daughter that God gave to me as a gift means much more to me than the loss of Facebook friends (not that they do not remain very close to my heart and always will.) Colleen and I were raised up under the same pastor/ teacher and so we are at the same place spiritually speaking; this has been a plus.

 My relationship with my spiritual daughter does not in any way infringe on my relationships with other women in my life who will always be near and dear to my heart; God doesn't divide His love; He multiplies it. And in no way does my relationship with her indicate that my life before she entered it was incomplete; I was (and always will be) beyond complete with my sons.

When God's plan for me and Colleen were orchestrated, everything on Facebook seemed to go back to normal and I, once again, began getting comments and greetings as before; it was just a pause of sorts.

This is what my darling daughter posted on Facebook thereafter: Mother (yes, everyone, she is my spiritual mother-supernaturally ordained by God.) I was so shocked with what I received in the mail today; a copy of my mother's book, "The First Strawberry Is Ripe." I loved your most tender heart -warming note inside the book. Now, to top it off, I got my wish, or I should say my prayer was answered. I received a beautiful picture of my mother. I must say, we do resemble each other a great deal. Oh, you made my day!!!! Thank you for taking the time to wrap up the book with loving care, and taking the time to go and mail it. It means so much to me all the time and effort you put into sending me those items. Now I must get the most beautiful frame. God will lead me to the perfect one. I'm in the middle of reading three books...one for my health so I will begin reading that book around the second week of March. I"m so excited!!!!!!! Thank you with all my heart. Love you special!!! (((HUGS))) Wow, I"m honored to know an author. I"m reading the back of your book. ♥♥ I just read Longing To Be A Bride. How beautiful. I need to put the book down as I need to turn off this computer. I think I'll read a couple of stories a day.

I saved this note from colleen. It will always be very special.

CHRISTINE'S E-MAILS

I have decided not to include any of Christine's e-mails to me because I am afraid that doing so will cause her to stop sending me them for fear of having them published; yet, I must make brief mention of how wonderfully they build me up on a consistent basis. God has given us a kindred spirit and her friendship is a beautiful gift to me.

RACHAEL'S TEXTS

The texts I get from my dear Rachael every week keep her very near and dear to my heart. Whether she is asking for my prayers for her little boys; for God's will on a matter or whatever the prayer may be; her coveting my prayers honors me and makes me feel included in her life. We are far apart these days, yet all we have to do is to call each other infrequently and we pick up where we left off. She is a gift to me.

CONNIE

Connie and I go way back. She still sends me homemade cards and prefers to write letters rather than to make a phone call which is alright because it's great to receive letters in snail mail. Next to Johnny Depp I am her favorite celebrity…heehee. Her craft room is all decorated with

Johnny Depp pictures which gives you a peek into her young spirit--the spirit that she imparts to me to keep me young. She is special to me.

SO MANY FRIENDS

Lifelong friends Linda and Muggs, and the rest of my friends: both Helens, Jim, Ellie, Pastor Sheff and Kim, David and Rachael, Pastor Wally and Kathy, Pastor Ron and Joyce, Ric, Steve, Edith, Heather, Bev, Ronda, Tom and Barbara, Tim and Diane, Pastor Colby and Dottie, Mike and Dottie, Linda, Bill and Chris, Mary, Denise, Vikki, Norma, Steve and Rhonda, Marian and all the rest, too numerous to mention…I love you all and thank God for each one of you. I love and appreciate all my Facebook friends, as well. I thank God for placing them all in my life.

CHAPTER 20

GOD'S IMPECCABLE TIMING

THE BOTTLE MAN

One day when I went to the market I dropped off bottles at the bottle return. The three bottle machines printed out three papers which stated how much credit I had coming. I thanked the bottle man for his help, and tucked the papers in my wallet making a mental note to retrieve them when I went through the check- out line.

After I finished loading the cart with groceries, I made my way to the check- out line where I started to load them onto the conveyor belt. I never gave a thought to the three credit slips in my wallet until I recognized the elderly man from the bottle return section of the store who came into the store and positioned himself at the check-out I was at the very second I got there and began bagging groceries. It was so obvious that the Holy Spirit had established the man's steps. I think we all know what a lousy feeling it is when we get home from the market, and realize that we forgot to redeem money- off coupons and such. That could easily have happened to me had I arrived home before realizing it.

I love when God does things like this.

PERFECT TIMING

I figured that I would miss the Fourth of July fireworks in 2013 because I had moved just a couple of weeks before, and I was still pretty busy and extremely tired at night. One night I prepared to sleep on my living room floor where it was nice and cool as the air in my bedroom was heavy as my a/c/ unit was still in my car trunk. I had to pull down the shades in the living room and dinette so that no one could see in. As I pulled down the shade in the dinette, the first blast of fireworks from across the way streamed high into the sky lighting it up with an array of beautiful designs followed by a big bang---more fireworks followed---orange spider ones, sparkly yellow ones, pink and green ones, wigglers, the ones that shoot up like rockets and those ones that resemble tadpoles that fall very slowly from the sky. God waited for the exact second that He knew I would be at the window for this to happen. I was like a 3 year-old clapping and shouting with joy as if the fireworks display was being put on just for me...what a Dad!!!!

PASTOR DIVINE

I sent a message to someone on Facebook one day to respond to the person's post and to tell her that she brought to mind someone I met years earlier, Pastor Divine from Africa. Two days later I found 25 of my steno books from years earlier at the bottom of a wicker chest. My large screen T.V was on the chest for a few years so I did not have access to whatever I had stored in there so I was in for a big treat, a monsoon of memories. I picked up one of the stenos to browse through, and on the second page there was an entry I recorded from Pastor Divine's message that he preached at my church when he visited the small Towson, Maryland church I attended at the time.

Most people would brush a happening such as this as happenstance, but I can't; to me God arranged that to happen.

HIATAL HERNIA

One night I was awakened at 2:45 a.m. with severe chest pains from a hiatal hernia which mimics a heart attack. Even though I have experienced these pains intermittently all through life, I couldn't help but wonder if it was the real thing, and if I was staring death in the face. But then God took over and I did an about face. I started singing in my spirit, 'I have a living Hope....I have a future...God has a plan for me...of this I'm sure, of this I'm sure....Jesus, You're my firm foundation etc...' the line, ' I have a future', totally released me from my worries...Satan is a defeated foe.....

THE FOX

One late Tuesday afternoon going on 5 o'clock I went outside to wait for Kathy, my pastor's wife, to pick me up for a prayer meeting at our friend Jan's house a couple of town's away. I thought I would walk all the way down to the main road to meet her so that she wouldn't have to drive all the way down into my complex. I knew that I couldn't walk that far without a problem, and I sensed that God was telling me that, but I was going to try anyway walking slowly. I got as far as the end of the sidewalk outside my house and turned to go left when I spotted a fox just about to walk across the street right where I was headed. The critter heard me and stopped in its tracks, looked toward me and starred me down for roughly three whole minutes.

I immediately sensed that God orchestrated that fox to appear exactly when I would have attempted the long walk to the main road. And I sensed that he ordered the fox to stand in the road for the long duration so that I would not attempt to continue walking if it ran into the woods.

Neither the fox nor I budged. I then thought to myself, what am I doing here? That fox could be rabid. I quickly turned around and hurried to my car where I sat to wait for my ride. God had His way.

WHAT WERE THE CHANCES?

One early afternoon after a long, stressful morning, I was prompted to drop everything and to go for my daily walk then and not to wait until my usual time. I knocked on my neighbor's door and she went with me.

As we passed the clubhouse some people were walking to their cars and waving to me. I recognized someone whom I had met a few weeks prior and her husband coming from the weekly Bible study and getting into their van. I knew that she had been wanting her husband to meet me so I went over and greeted them with holy hugs--the timing was perfect--all God.

ELLIE'S VISIT

My friend Ellie lost her job and in between job interviews she drove down from two hours north to visit me for the day. Her visit fell on the same day that a friend ended our friendship and the loss was playing heavily on my mind; I could not get over the timing. Ellie talked for several hours sharing burdens that were bottled up for decades. I guess you might say that God was killing two birds with one stone; she was getting a much needed release and God was sparing me from being left alone with my emotions when going through something extremely painful.

Ad lib: I guess I should say that God killed three birds with one stone (so to speak--I know that God would never kill a bird.) I had a colonoscopy the day before Elle's visit. I had to lie on a gurney on my left side during the procedure. I was O.K. that afternoon, but the following day, the day of Ellie's visit, the pain was terrible. I could barely walk to the bathroom. Had I not had company I would not have taken time to sit comfortably which would have caused worse pain…connect the dots…

GO NOW! (1)

Just a couple of weeks after moving that last time, the Holy Spirit said to drop everything and go to the complex Laundromat right away; I complied. A neighbor woman, Beverly, was there waiting for her clothes to finish washing. We started talking. I mentioned to her that I live only eight minutes away from my church. She told me that she attends South Waterboro Bible church. "I know exactly where that us. It's right across the street from my church". We talked some more and she said, "I just prayed and asked God yesterday to send me a Christian friend to this complex, and He answered my prayer by having me meet you".

GO NOW (2)

A few weeks after my last move, I was walking along the sidewalk to my apartment after going to the community room to pick up my mail when I saw an elderly woman sitting out on her patio. I waved and started to walk up her long walkway to pay her a visit. She hollered out, "I'm not who you think I am". (She must have thought that I thought her to be the lady who lived next door to her.) "I'm coming to say hello to you no matter who you are", I answered. I introduced myself. She told me that her name was Kate. We chatted for a bit and then another neighbor came over and joined us.

Little did I know that within a couple of weeks Kate would no longer be able to sit on her patio. I heard from her nearest neighbor that she was full of cancer and stayed in bed most of the time. During the next few weeks I met some of her granddaughters who left their homes and kids to stay with their grandmother. I asked them if I could go over and read to their grandmother from the Bible or to just visit with her for a short while. They discouraged me. I asked my prayer group to pray with me that God would make a way for me to get to her with the gospel before she passed.

Then one day when her granddaughters were heading back to their own homes and families, I hugged them and told them how special they were for giving to their grandmother so selflessly, when one of them told me to go knock on the door and to go in and read to Kate from the Bible. The next morning I wrapped some homemade brownies in foil and headed to her place. The old woman met me at the door, but would not allow me to go inside.

'Oh Lord, what can I do now? It seems like I'm at a dead end'.

Two days later while walking passed Kate's house I had a light bulb moment. I thought about taking her a book of Godly poems and about writing her a note. I went home and did so including writing down my telephone number and telling to call me if she needed anything.

Just a few nights after that my assistant pastor, Ron and his wife Joyce, dropped me off out in front of my house after church, when a relative of Kate's (whom I had never met) came running out of Kate's house and called to me. She said she went to my house looking for me after reading the card and poems I left on the door, and just missed me earlier. Kate had either a massive heart attack or stroke that morning and was unresponsive. The family wanted me to go over the next morning to read to her from the Bible. They believed she would hear me even if she was in a coma (and, of course, I believed that too having been a hospice volunteer.) The relative told me that my lovely note and book of poetry meant so much to Kate and that she kept it on her bedside table.

The following morning I was thinking of going to Kate's house after my 10 o'clock car appointment, but God said authoritatively, 'go right now', so I went over at 9:30. The relative grabbed me by the arm and practically pulled me into the bedroom. Kate was in her last moments. I began to rub her arms and to minister Christ's love to her, ushering her into heaven and praying. The relative asked me to recite the Lord's Prayer; she joined me in reciting it. Kate passed away as I was praying. I wasn't there for more than two minutes when she passed. God kept her alive until I got there. Her relative and I felt that it was so timely and so special. Her relative told me that Kate let her know that she was a believer before she had the massive stroke. Praise God.

It was only because of all the prayers of the saints that I was able to pray with her before she went.

BEYOND IMPECCABLE

At a Wednesday evening service at my church, my pastor, Pastor Wally, gave the introduction and asked my assistant pastor, Pastor Ron, to deliver the message. The verse that Pastor Wally spoke on was Joshua 1:5, 'As I was with Moses, so I will be with you'.

When I arrived home after the church service, I hurried into my apartment to turn on my computer so that I could tune into my Baltimore church service being aired live on the Internet. It took a few minutes for the little blue circle to stop turning around. As soon as I accessed the Baltimore church service my Baltimore pastor was quoting Joshua 1:5, 'As I was with Moses, so I will be with you'…the exact same verse Pastor Wally spoke on at our church service in Maine.

I COULD HARDLY BELIEVE IT

After moving to Southern Maine in 2013, I ordered custom made, wooden blinds for my living room window…something I have wanted for a very long time. After they were installed I wasn't able to use the cords to pull them all the way down to the window sill for some reason. I wasn't bothered by it though because I had two air conditioners in the windows and pulling the blinds just half way down worked out fine. But when fall rolled around and the air conditioners were packed away in storage I had the maintenance man and two neighbors try to pull down the blinds; yet, they could not. I was going to call the manufacturer in California, but I figured I'd play around with them some more which I did several times. I tried pulling the cords sideways like I read in the directions and all sorts of things.

Then early one evening after I had spent the whole day on producing a show; burning discs to send to my T.V. stations; writing and serving the Body of Christ; not even allowing myself a break, the Holy Spirit whispered to me that He was going to direct me in how to get the blinds down. I went to the window and gripped the bunch of slats with my left hand and pulled on the cord with my right hand tugging the slats as I did and they moved about a quarter of an inch. I then did it again and again and again until they reached the window sill. It was simple as pie.

For over three months dozens of efforts were made by a number of people to accomplish what I accomplished that evening. The reason being was that until that very moment the timing wasn't right. God chose a time when I was physically and mentally exhausted to bless me beyond/beyond.

THE ECLIPSE

October 18, 2013. I watched the movie, 'Joshua, The Battle of Jericho' on Netflix. It ended at 7:50 p.m. I then got on the computer and went to Facebook to check out the newsfeed. My granddaughter-in-law, Barbara, from Connecticut had posted for everyone in the east to look at the moon in ten minutes at 7:50 p.m. to check out the eclipse. I looked at the clock. It was 7:50 p.m. right on the dot. I quickly ran outside and looked up at the moon to see the event right in the nick of time.

REARRANGED SCHEDULE

I tried to get on Facebook three times one Saturday morning and couldn't so I delved into other things instead. I videoed a show, uploaded it, burned 13 D.V.D.'s, labeled mailers and got all set for the following week. The second I tried to get on Facebook after I completed my work, I was able to get on. All Daddy! He led me to get my work done ahead of time so that I could have the whole weekend to do whatever and to relax.

{"cl_impid":"4bfa4	€,´,€,´,水,?,?	AQA4qEo-	{"actor":"107085!
1	1	AQCMbcdfonG9	

CHAPTER 21

39 TIMES

A GYPSY FOR JESUS

He goes before us....

Some families never change their address in their lifetime; others move once or twice; military families relocate habitually; career people often relocate to different parts of the country or world as they are advanced in companies; and then there are Christians like me who are gypsies for Jesus whom the Lord uproots and transplants even more than military families. When I moved from Warren, Maine down the coast to Brunswick, my 38th move, I thought I had died and gone to heaven because my second son and his wife lived just a few miles away, and their adult kids and grandkids lived in the same college town in close proximity to me. My third son and his wife lived one town over. After living 600 miles away from all of them for 10 years, and 60 miles away from them for over four years, it was unimaginable to think that I was going to be a part of a family again, and that I would have loved ones nearby and could die in peace.

pg. 211

Wrong....

From the day after I moved into my Brunswick apartment I knew that I would only be passing through. The old familiar passages of Scriptures that spoke about dwelling temporarily in certain places showed up on day number two, and began to increasingly emerge before my eyes making God's intentions totally unmistakable to me once again. I totally understand what many people think about God's unconventional ways of leading His flock. None of it makes any sense, but it is not supposed to make earthly sense; it is only supposed to make divine sense.

I had been traveling down the Maine Turnpike to Biddeford, a 50 minute trip, every other Sunday to attend church. Spending such a brief amount of time with others that were reared up in the same ministry as me was definitely inadequate; I craved for a lot more fellowship. My former pastor's monthly visits to Brunswick, at which time we put on concerts in the community room where I lived, were wonderful and uplifting; yet, did not take the place of actual fellowship.

I had become so accustomed to packing and unpacking, planning, changing addresses and all the rest that I just plummeted into the mode like a robot each time. The 38th time, however, was tough on the old body, and I did have some genuine concerns about whether I would be physically able to go through it again.

Filling out applications and calling management companies toyed with my sanity time and again; yet, the grace of God went before me with each form I filled out. Driving a long distance to potential apartment complexes presented monotony and restlessness at times. Trusting God for the unknown, however, and remembering what He had done through previous moves brought excitement and anticipation that He would do it again. Downsizing... 'Here I go again,' I said to myself. I looked around and told myself that I had so little left from which to downsize; yet, I realized how much I had compared with many of the world's people.

It was difficult breaking the news to my family again. I thought one of my sons would have me committed. And then I sat back and waited... Well, I didn't exactly sit back; I wrote another book. I did not feel led of God to call the management companies to see how far I was from the top of the lists. I was not at all interested in moving in the winter anyway, so I made no effort to speed up the process.

Toward my ninth month in the new apartment, God began to speak more loudly as well as more frequently concerning another move. By that time I realized that I had served God's purpose in getting a monthly Christian concert established in Brunswick, and it was time for Him to use me in other places. One thing I became cognizant of was that I was starving for physical fellowship with the Body of Christ. Yes, I sometimes got together with other knowledgeable Christians, and I was often in the company of nominal Christians that were more into philosophy than the Bible, but we all know what it is to gravitate toward our own kind. I needed fellowship with others who spoke the same spiritual language as me. I was listening for that certain sound.

God always goes before us. God's angels met Abraham on his journey. God was hurling similar verses at me left and right. When God called Jacob to go back to his land, he put his wives on camels and let his livestock go. Can you imagine! That had to be like taking a knife in his heart. I can't imagine having to let my animals go, not that I have any, but if I did. I believe that God was telling me not to take everything with me, but to downsize, yet again.

God gave me a really neat verse, Luke 20:16, about removing the tenants and giving the vineyard to others. I interpreted it to mean that God was going to remove certain tenants from an apartment and give their apartment to me. He has done that before so I had every reason to believe that He would do it again. He also gave me Acts 7-3, "Leave this country and your family and go to a land where I will show you", and its sister verse from the Old Testament Genesis 12:1, "Leave thy country and thy kindred and go to a land where I will show you".

In between Scriptural gleanings pertaining to my move, I scouted the potential new area with my granddaughter a couple of times. Because my granddaughter lived in Kennebunk, I thought that I would like to live there too. But God had other plans and this is the way He gave me His mind on it. For three days I could not stop singing the stanza of a song I had been practicing, 'Keep Me In Your Will'. I finally said, "Lord, what are you trying to say to me?" I then put my C.D. of the song into the

C.D. player and got a paper and pen. I pressed the play button and prepared to write the words of the song and to heed what God wanted to say to me; I was all ears. And there it was: 'Put me where You want to, not where I want to be.' I was pierced; it stung. I cried my eyes out. I wanted desperately to be in Kennebunk near my granddaughter; yet, God did not want me there; I trusted Him. I gave my up desire to Him on the spot.

(Months later God revealed to me one of His reasons for not wanting me to move to Kennebunk; my granddaughter ended up moving someplace else; I would have been down there by myself.)

As He has done in the past when nudging me to move, God had caused increased noise around my house such as gun shots going off on summer nights; noise from wild parties in the neighborhood and more; I got the hint. Kinda reminded me of one time when He wanted me to move and I was so comfortable where I was that I was slow about making plans to relocate. The noise in my building escalated and the final annoyance was when my upstairs neighbors positioned their barbeque grille right outside my picture window in my living room. I was upset that they stooped so low; yet, I knew that God was behind it just to push me out of there.

Contrary to what one might imagine pertaining to moving to different ministry localities, the moves are not always upscale. A few of my moves took me from bigger, lovelier apartments than the ones to which I moved. The natural person would question God as to how He could allow things like that to happen, but when you and God are a team and one in Spirit, you just trust.

God gave me some interesting thoughts and verses on moving as one who is called to do so. They are as follows:

Break up uncultivated ground. Go where ground has not been broken before. My church has only 15 regular people in attendance not counting children;

 The area is wide open for the gospel;

Do not sow amongst thorns. If you have been ministering in a community that is primarily against born-again believers or evangelism,

God may be telling you as He has told me in the past to stop sowing amongst thorns. Remember that if we are in the place that God calls us, He will send his anointing. That is why we must obey Him and follow Him to His perfect geographical place for us. So I haven't lived in some places for a full year; what business is that of mine? I am to obey and follow Him and stop rationalizing. He goes ahead of us to pave the way. I will throw in here that none of my moves had anything to do with inability to pay my rent. Once I had an injury and couldn't work and was threatened with eviction, but God brought in the money and I did pay my rent and got squared away. It has come to my attention that a story is going around that the reason I may move so many times may be because of problems paying my rent...not true;

We need to get pregnant with that for which we pray. If we pray that God will use us in many places, what better way to do that than to lead us to meet more people in more neighborhoods? We need to embrace our call;

It's ours...we should claim what is ours.

After filling out applications and talking to people in rental offices and being told it could be a 2- 5 year wait, God told me that he could rearrange that; He blew me away. He also gave me Song of Solomon 1:8, "...follow the shepherd's tents"...this is indicative of following the pastor to whom He was sending me.

The waiting started to make me a little nuts after awhile. It was the dead of winter so I barricaded myself in the house and went full speed ahead on my manuscript; I was on a roll. Thoughts kept coming to mind faster than a speeding train. In less time than ever I had almost completed a book---all except the part where God would be moving me. It started to press on my mind again.

One Sunday morning I was feeling sluggish so I prayed about whether I should cancel my plans to head up the coast to visit my pastor friend as it was my alternate week from heading south to Biddeford. I definitely felt led to stay home that morning so at 10:15 a.m. I called my pastor's wife at church to see if her son-in-law would hook me up to the church computer so that I could listen to my new pastor's message from home by way of the phone. It was because of that decision that God was able to give me definition concerning my move, the definition for which I had waited desperately. My pastor announced that after much prayer he had decided to move the location of our church to the town where he lived. He conducted a vote and they even considered my hand as a raised hand even though I was on the other end of the phone and not present with them.

This news meant that God would move me to an entirely different area-- probably within five miles of my pastor and his wife--so cool. I looked on the net to see about senior apartments in their area and lo and behold there was a complex five minutes away from them. And talk about impeccable timing; God did not bring this information to me until I finished my manuscript because my mind would not have been able to handle writing a book at the same time that I would pack to move and go through everything that moving entails.

The next morning I woke up dreaming that I was taking care of a newborn baby. I was ecstatically happy; I'd never been so happy in all of my life. People around me in the dream were remarking that they had never seen me so happy. It seemed that I was right in my element with that newborn baby. Now to put this story in reverse---do you remember me sharing with you that God gave me a series of dreams about being pregnant and about giving birth and gave me the interpretation that it spoke of new life --something new in my life? The latest dream depicted the new life of which He spoke. It was a culmination of all the dreams He had given me. My moving would be the fulfillment of His plan for me.

My friend called to tell me that there was a brand new medical facility and a new market in the town to which, more than likely, I would be moving. That information removed some fears that cropped up; yet, I was still being plagued with the area being so rural. That plague came from out of nowhere since I had lived in rural areas many times over. It seemed as if having been only a five minute drive from the malls and stores in Brunswick spoiled me.

Not only that, however; I kept thinking that I was being demoted. I had been in an assembly with over 1,500 hundred people; then went to one with 60 people then there I was placed in assembly of a dozen people. And if that wasn't discouraging enough, God was sending me to the boonies. What was up with that!

God saw deeper into my soul than I could have imagined. One Sunday at church God spoke through my pastor's vocal chords and addressed the seeming dilemma. The pastor talked about the small room that he and others were building in his barn which we would use for a small church. His emphasis was that throughout Biblical history God used this pattern to test and to reward His people. I cried inside with humble appreciation knowing that our small group was chosen to bring glory to God. It made me proud to be on the bandwagon.

In the course of my move, God, in His goodness, gave me a rhema from heaven. He gave it to me through a message that one of my pastors preached from the pulpit at the Baltimore church, and I received it by way of the Internet. He shared a story of his early years in the ministry and how that he went to our founding pastor and asked, "Is there something wrong with me?" He went on to tell the pastor that every time he moved someplace he could not stay in that place for very long before he got itching to go someplace else. The pastor told him it was because he had a gift of evangelism.

I was preparing to move for my 39th time and just before I heard that message preached, I had asked God the same thing that the pastor asked our founding pastor: "Is something wrong with me?" I was itching to move on in the same way. God spoke to me through the head pastor's words: 'You have a gift of evangelism'. That resonated with me because in my younger days when I was physically able to evangelize (before my back became worse), I loved passing out tracts and sharing the gospel on the streets. To find me in a park or on the streets was to capture me in 'my element'. I positively loved street witnessing for Christ.

God's rhema to me was exceedingly timely and 'right on' not only blessing me, but putting spring in my steps. I had worked hard in the last town I lived in nurturing the Body of Christ, and it was time for me to move on—time to break up uncultivated ground (as the Bible puts it). Where He was leading me I would follow.

pg. 217

Now how is this for more impeccable timing? I received the news of the apartment I would rent just a couple of days after I started using a tens unit for back pain. There was no way that I would have been able to pack without the unit. God's timing was perfect.

Seven people besides me were interested in the apartment in southern Maine, the apartment that I fell in love with 30 seconds after I went inside; yet, as much as I loved it I would not have been disappointed if another person was picked to move there because of my complete trust in God. I wanted what He wanted for me –nothing else. It was funny…a relative of whom I was a houseguest asked me about the apartment. I told her that seven other people wanted it as well. She said, 'you don't have much of a chance'. I answered: "If God wants me there I'll be there". The next day her phone rang and it was my son calling to say that the management company called his house and left a message for me as I did not have cell phone service in Connecticut. "Tell my mom that she got the rent". My relative was just as excited as I. I cut my out of town trip short and headed home to begin the next leg of my other journey.

I took my time packing taking many breaks. I allowed myself one week before the move to get together with friends and to leave time for the unexpected. It was wonderful getting together for a barbeque with neighbors and being treated to breakfast, lunch and dinner by friends. Everyone made me feel so loved. The greatest compliment I received was this: "With over a hundred women living in our complex there is always something being said about people. I want to tell you that you are well liked by everyone here. No one has ever said a negative word against you or gossiped about you. Everyone has always had positive things to say about you". I give God the glory for that statement.

GOD SAVED THE BEST TILL LAST….

The new apartment is an end unit, something for which I have desired for a long time. The lawn extends from the front of the house, all along the side of the house and around back covering at least two acres, but the acreage is adjacent to much more acreage belonging to a big, farm house up the street making it appear unbelievably spacious. Several huge spruce trees are spaced evenly throughout the backyard. Upon viewing those for the first time I immediately visualized them covered with snow in the wintertime. What an amazing sight that would be.

The rooms in the new place are situated so that I can't hear anyone snoring during the night; I can't hear the T.V. next door blaring preventing me from having the pleasure of reading a book; I can't hear neighbors walking around. Yahoo! The living room is so big for a senior apartment that to me it looked like a dance hall when I first moved in. I had to position one of my sofas diagonally to fill in some space to make it look smaller and homier.

The whole apartment was flooded when pipes burst a few months earlier; therefore, the whole apartment was remodeled with brand new beige wall to wall carpeting. Brand new kitchen cabinets were installed. New wooden flooring was laid. In former apartments I was the only tenant who got stuck with everything old when all the other tenants got new stuff. That caused me to be even more grateful for the blessings.

MOVING DAY...

Three of my sons showed up bright and early to move me with a rental truck, a dolly and moving blankets. Tony came all the way up from Connecticut to help. Their grandfather was a mover and they picked up many of his techniques when they were younger. When the truck was loaded they went on ahead to the new apartment to start unloading while I finished packing some light, last minute belongings in my car.

Driving the one hour and 10 minutes gave me a chance to catch my breath. When I arrived the truck was almost completely unloaded. My sons repositioned furniture to where I wanted things placed. Things could not have gone more smoothly. My guys had to head out as each of them had plans for the day. I puttered around until late afternoon when I had to head back to the old apartment to sleep over as I had a walk through inspection the following morning.

After the inspection my fourth son showed up after traveling for five hours. Although I was disappointed that he was not there the preceding day with his brothers, it was more than obvious to me that it was God's design for him to arrive when he did. For the next four days at the new place, my son rearranged everything for me; he packed the storage area labeling my boxes and bags; he put dishes and kitchenware into cupboards for me; he put together my desk; he hung curtain rods and curtains; he spent many an hour cleaning up my computer and installing a much better virus protection program on it than the one I had. He did everything that needed to be done after the actual move. He and I took rides to explore the new area each afternoon and grabbed some lunch in nearby towns. It gave us a chance for the two of us to catch up. Things could not have gone more perfectly.

A few months later he came back to visit and we picked up where we had left off exploring many additional areas, going to the lake, watching movies and doing what we enjoy most which is to converse about numerous subjects.

TWO AIR CONDITIONERS...

It was pretty hot in my apartment. My a/c unit was in storage at my son's house. I had him put it in my car one day when I was visiting him. Little did I know that one of the accordion pieces on the side of the unit was missing. I asked the maintenance man if he could use a piece of cardboard to put it in my dinette window. His response was: "If I spent the time cutting out cardboard to install yours and 100 other units I would never get any of my other work done". So the saga began.

I was on the phone with a national chain trying to order the part on line. They wanted to charge me more for the accordion piece than I paid for the whole unit. Then I was on the phone calling local hardware and appliances stores. All the time I was sweating bullets. I finally got the piece from my former neighbor who had an extra air conditioner. I hired someone other than the maintenance man to put in the unit. After all that the unit did not work properly.

In the meantime a Facebook friend whose daughter goes to my former church messaged me that she was cleaning out her garage since her husband had unexpectedly passed away, and she had three air conditioners that she wanted to give away. I took two of them. My former pastor put them in his car trunk when she visited his church, and he and his wife met me at a MacDonald's parking lot in a nearby town when they were heading south on the turnpike and switched a/c units from his trunk to my trunk.

What a divine Provider!

BLESSINGS AT THE NEW HOUSE...

A neighbor whom I met in the community room was very friendly. She told me how that she goes for kidney dialysis three mornings a week. The first thing I thought of was that the ladies from my church have a prayer shawl ministry knitting and crocheting shawls, and giving them away to the people at local dialysis centers so that the patients could warm themselves in the cool rooms at the centers. I asked if they would give me one to give to my new neighbor. They obliged. They wrapped the beautiful shawl in pretty paper and placed it in a big, party bag decorated with ribbons. They wrote my neighbor a lovely note putting it inside the bag. I walked down to Diana's and presented it to her. I wish they could have been there with me to witness my neighbor's excitement.

The new neighbors nearest to me have been absolute sweethearts. Several younger neighbors at the other end of the complex welcomed me and showed extreme kindness by helping me out with some things in my apartment, and by checking to see if I was alright when the humidity was at a dangerously high level.

Blessings galore came my way from the moment I moved to the new property. I needed to come up with $390.00 for two fillings in my teeth, and depended upon the return of my security deposit from the former rent to pay the dentist. I never expected the return of the whole amount; yet, I received it all totaling $394.81 almost to the dollar of the amount I needed. Money gifts which I had saved from the preceding Christmas covered the activation charges for the new accounts I took on. I did what I do best when some new bill would hit me square between the eyes: I trusted God. He had always come through before and would again. I reminded myself that the bills were His bills and not mine.

I hit pay dirt at every yard sale I went to purchasing a like-new file cabinet for only $3.00; a Chinese black screen with six Chinese ladies and crafted with mother of pearl which would enhance my Chinese decor for only $1.00; wicker shelves purchased at a thrift shop and a few more odds and ends brightened up the place. The burgundy matting on the beautiful painting that my girlfriend gave me contrasted so much with the black, fuchsia and pea green shades in my living room that I had to do something. God gave me a simple and inexpensive solution to match the coloring. I used a black magic marker to color over the burgundy matting, and then I used one container of silver, glitter glue purchased at the dollar store for 3/$1.00, and dragged the tip along the whole matting making a wiggly design around the whole painting. Walla…it not only matched my coloring; it was even prettier than it was before I made the changes.

Early on I was blessed with lots of company. My daughter-in-law, granddaughter and great-granddaughter came down to see me on the train. My son drove down in his car to meet them and to take me out for breakfast. My other son and his wife drove down. My former neighbors drove down to spend time with me. My former camping neighbors drove down to visit me. My pastor, an accomplished carpenter, came to help with a project. His wife came to help with another project.

My new place is several miles away from everything, yet the city I shop in is only a 10 minute drive from my house. There are country stores all around me in closer proximity to my house. There are at least three lakes in close proximity, as well. The post office, a facility which I patronize quite frequently because of my work, is situated right down the road. My house is exceptionally easy to find, a straight shot from the highway with only one turn.

I wasn't situated in my brand new apartment for more than three days when I had a knock at my front door. The visitors were my assistant pastor and his wife, Pastor Ron and Joyce, who came to welcome me to the area. What a wonderful surprise! We had the sweetest fellowship and the pastor shared many wonderful portions from the Word of God. He brought such illumination to Bible stories that I had read many times over, yet never fully understood. We had a special time of prayer before they left.

The following week they came bearing a peck of fresh picked strawberries. Again we discussed many subjects related to God and the Bible. The berries were juicy and succulent. After their visit I washed them, sliced them and sprinkled them with sugar and a little water and covered them and refrigerated them overnight. The next day they were perfect to serve with short cakes and whipped cream.

The visits have continued a couple of times a month and so have the gifts of food included fresh picked blueberries during blueberry season and fresh picked apples during apple season. But more than the goodies the rich food from heaven from seasoned Christians continuously enlarges my heart. God's people feed each other spiritually when they get together, plus we arm each other with the armor of God when we come together, so with each visit from the Body of Christ I become stronger and more fulfilled.

I continue to coordinate concerts at my former complex utilizing that time to spend overnights with my kids in that area. The concerts are so enjoyable and not only afford me the opportunity to see my old friends and family, but concert goers look forward to them.

It is so wonderful to be established once again in a church which is a branch ministry of my larger world-wide church. It is rewarding to once again speak the same spiritual language as my brethren, and to hear that certain sound from one another. My pastor's wife insisted on picking me up for church after the time change, and after we had to turn the clocks back an hour as she didn't want me to drive after dark. Knowing what a busy person she is, I accepted the offer of the assistant pastor and his wife instead. Our lives are interwoven because of the small size of the church.

Maybe God is calling you to change jobs. Maybe He wants you to move to follow His call. Maybe you love your job and your initial thoughts after hearing from Him are not good ones, but you quickly make a decision to trust God and to obey Him. Maybe you are a part of God's plan and He wants to bring about reconciliation in your life. Maybe you are resisting Him. Maybe you are tempted to hold onto your stubbornness, but the Holy Spirit won't let you have peace and you become cognizant of what the devil is doing in your emotions and you give it up. You ask God to go before you and you bring Him glory by following Him, by reconciling (if that is the case) and you end up being the recipient of happiness and peace beyond your understanding. Called out ones have something in common; they are under scrutiny by the Holy Spirit. If they are using their eyes, ears or mouth for something that is not pleasing to God, they experience instant conviction. They recognize God in everything. If something seems coincidental, they know that it is not.

They are extremely cognizant of the end times and that sinners need to be saved before Christ comes back or they will face an eternity in hell. Called out ones have a heart for souls and pray frequently for the lost. The Word says that when more is given to a person more is expected of that person. Called out ones expect to make plenty of sacrifices for God's kingdom. Their time is no longer their own. Just like the old country doctors who refused to go home after hours until all their scheduled patients, and all the ones who showed up with no appointment who had to be squeezed in were all taken care of. Called out ones put all those in need and all the ones God brings to them every day at all hours in front of themselves and minister unceasingly. They give money to the hurting out of their own needs. In return they are given treasures--large doses of divine favor, honor, endless storehouses in their soul, storehouses of wisdom and knowledge, storehouses of God's secrets. They are given a keen sensitivity to hear from the Lord, and they possess God's anointing. They are given a tremendous amount of blessings. They are given dreams and visions which are the ultimate joy in this life.

Anyone who has been called out spends an enormous amount of time studying. They keep God's principles on their heart. "They keep His teaching as the apple of their eye", Proverbs 7:1. "You speak excellent and princely things and the opening of your lips shall be for right things", Proverbs 8:6, "How much better to get skillful and Godly wisdom than gold?" Proverbs 16:16. "That I may cause those who love Me to inherit true riches and that I may fill their treasuries", Proverbs 8:21.

Called out ones are concerned as the Apostle Paul was in Romans 10:1 that souls might be saved, and like others who have gone before us we are willing to make fools of ourselves for Christ's sake.

If you are a Christian contemplating moving consider these words that God gave to me:

"Break up uncultivated ground; do not sow amongst thorns," Hosea 10:12...

Remember that if we are in the place that God calls us, God sends His anointing, and He goes ahead of us to pave the way...

Get pregnant with what you pray for...

Embrace the call; it's yours--claim it...

This is what I have chosen to do. Whether I see the results of my work in my lifetime does not matter. I must do what I was called to do.

EPILOGUE

God has revealed to me further not to despise the day of small things. I have been continually astonished that my testimonies have branched out farther and wider than I could have imagined. Having gone years with minimal feedback, I am now hearing from people all over the globe remarking on how they have been blessed and personally affected by them.

I have picked up one additional T.V. station covering a large city and 15 towns; that would bring the total number of towns covered to over 60; that represents more than a scant number of people. I covet everyone's prayers not only for viewers, but for viewers who will let God's message transform their lives.

I expect that the size of the congregation of the church I attend will increase, or that other house churches will pop up as smaller congregations can create a warmer atmosphere for newcomers. I have heard people say that they have been going to a large assembly for as long as 15 years; yet, the pastor and those with positions did not know their names. That is sad. It tells me that something is missing. God wants us to be members, in particular, in the Body of Christ.

When a radio station played a Halloween joke on Americans in 1938 announcing that Martians had landed in New Jersey killing numbers of people, scores of Americans went into mass hysteria. The broadcast, instigated by Orson Wells, a famous radio personality, was also responsible for a national wringing of hands causing many to commit suicide, and many to lose their lives as a result of accidents due to a mass exodus. Millions across the country thought they were going to die that night. Scores of people headed away from the center of the city toward the water to try to save themselves from possible explosions, the same way they did in New York City on the day of 9/11. Masses were fearful; masses turned to God like never before. It is my belief that our T.V. stations will interrupt programs to bring forth emergency broadcasts publicizing attacks on our cities all over the world in an increased rate in the next few years, only, unlike the 1938 event, the future emergency broadcasts will not be a joke. I believe that people will turn to God like never before. To whom else could they turn? My prayer is that my shows and books will be used to draw people closer to Him during those times and even after I am in heaven.

There is nothing that differentiates my testimonies to the seemingly small events that happen in everyone's lives on a daily basis except that I recognize God in everything.

It is mind-blowing that God could create the universe in such a profound way, and yet orchestrate events to take place in such simplistic ways in order to be a personal God to each of His children.

He is all in all...

QUOTES AND VERSES.....

Our life is a life, not a duty…

The Bible is a message, not a book…

He saved you from the guttermost to the uttermost…

We don't pray to get answers from God; we pray to get God…

When we are around Jesus Christ all the time, we reflect His glory all the time…

Our time with Him is not so much a visit as it is a homecoming…

Experience must be balanced by caution….

Good news nourishes our bones, Proverbs 15:30…

The Lord will perfect that which concerns me, Psalms 138:8…

We need guts to obey God, and not to have our emotions control us...

God closes our eyes until we pray…

He baptizes us in the Holy Spirit not with the Holy Spirit...

He gave us a free will, and He will not violate our free will…

He is under His own decree of justice (which keeps Him from doing certain things)…

He loves it that we are thinkers.

TO HELL AND BACK

Most everyone on this planet questions the reality of heaven and hell at some point during his/her lifetime. I have always believed in heaven, but there was a time when I did not believe in hell. My reasoning was, 'how could a loving God send souls to a place of torment?' That was before I was taught. In the middle 70's when I was so bold as to denounce Jesus' words about a literal hell, I experienced the literal hell--- at least one section of it. I had either died from a severe asthma attack and woke up in hell, or I was translated there by God while awake. I have no memory of having a physical body, yet I was acutely conscious of my soul. I was suspended in outer darkness. I instantly knew where I was. I did not see any flames in the section of hell I was in, but that did not make hell any less horrific. I was suspended in a blacker than black atmosphere sensing a pronounced sense of falling, and consumed with fear. My senses were unfathomably heightened making me highly conscious of the black hole in which I was engulfed.

Hell was tormenting. It was 100 times scarier than any Alfred Hitchcock or Stephen King movie or any other science fiction movie that I had ever seen. I was cognizant that others were there also; yet, I was alone—dreadfully, unmistakably, alone. Communication with anyone else was impossible. The feeling of isolation was beyond unbearable! Words cannot describe the deafening solitude and loneliness.

Even worse than the isolation, the blackness and the horror was the absence of the presence of God and the absence of His love. The utter realization of the permanency of the abyss was a million times more profound than any desperate situation imaginable. The utter realization of the permanent separation from loved ones was a million times worse than any separation of which the human mind could conceive. Most of all, the utter realization of eternal separation from God was more than a trillion times more unbearable than any unbearable situation in which I have ever been.

God could not use me as a Christian witness if I did not believe in hell, and that is why He sent me to hell; I had to experience it first-hand to believe it.

I cannot close my eyes for even five seconds to allow myself to think about the experience in hell because the horror of remembering would cause me to go into hysterics even 40 plus years later. That is the reason that I kept the experience to myself for all those years.

In the early 2,000's a pastor I knew shared in a group meeting that many pastors were allowed the experience of going to hell in order that they could properly communicate God's message on hell to their congregations and to the world. In that same time period I started to hear about others who had similar experiences as mine. That was a confirmation to me that God was telling me that it was time for me to make my experience known.

Hell is real. Do not allow the devil to tell you that God is sadistic if He sends anyone there. He gave His only begotten Son to come to earth as a man, to identify with us, to endure terrible persecution and ultimately to be nailed to a cross and to die for the sins of men. Jesus came as a ransom for us. What more could God do to save us from eternal damnation? He did it all, He gave it all. He made eternal life available to all. His love for you is enormous. It is your choice whether you spend eternity in heaven or hell…nobody's but yours….please pass this on…

GOD LOVES YOU

The good news refers to the good news of the gospel which is that Christ came to die for us and to take care of the sin issue and to offer us eternal life. The facts that we always mess up and that our minds continually change have nothing to do with our ultimate decision to accept Christ as our Lord and Saviour. Those things will happen until we leave this earth. All that we need to do when these things happen is to rebound, confess our iniquities and ask for grace. It is not that grace gives us a license to sin, but when we do sin it covers us, and certainly, in that regard the love of God does not fail. No one goes to hell for doing bad things; no one goes to hell for murdering someone etc. The only reason a person goes to hell is for not receiving all that Jesus did to make salvation available to us. What I had to do years ago to understand it was to visualize my sons taking Christ's journey; being tortured and put to death in an agonizing way, and to have people jeer at them, spit on them and reject them. Personalizing it like that was when I got the full revelation of what Christ did. The enemy wants the world to think of God as a sadist--to think of Him as putting us here with no hope and looking at an eternity in hell if we don't receive His Son. Well, God's way of looking at it is this: Yes, we were born into the world not asking to be born; yet, because of His great love toward the world, He sent His Son as a ransom for us--every one of us, but He also gave us a free will because He didn't want us to feel like prisoners. This is love that goes beyond/beyond. This is love that gives us wings to fly.

A Christian believer needs a church just as a candle needs a candlestick, like a tree needs soil, and like an electric light bulb needs a socket. Without a candlestick a candle cannot stand; without soil a tree cannot grow; without a socket an electric bulb cannot shine; neither can you without fellowship. A Christian cannot stand, grow nor shine without a church.

If you have never asked Jesus Christ to come into your heart to live, please won't you consider doing that now? It is a heart issue. He is very near waiting for you to open your heart to Him. He cannot do it for you. You are the one who has to do it. You can kneel down or you can sit down. Just talk to God. Ask Him to take away all your sins. Thank Him for dying for you on the cross. Ask Him to indwell you and to help you to follow Him. Ask Him to fill you with peace and joy. You will instantly become a new person filled with the Holy Spirit of God, the third Person in the Trinity. Ask Him to direct you to a pastor/teacher who will instruct you in the ways of the Bible. And don't forget to read the Bible every day and to pray. I would recommend that those new in the faith to start reading not at the beginning of the Bible in the Book of Genesis, but in the gospels of Matthew, Mark, Luke and John, and then to read the Psalms, Proverbs and the New Testament before reading the Old Testament. When you are ready to embark on the Old Testament I would recommend that you read Genesis and Job and digest those books before delving into the other books. Happy reading...

Made in the USA
Charleston, SC
14 February 2014